I0815791

H Chris Ransford

The Science of Destiny

De Chardin's *Omega Point* and Beyond

H Chris Ransford

THE SCIENCE OF DESTINY

De Chardin's *Omega Point* and Beyond

Bibliographic information published by the Deutsche Nationalbibliothek
Die Deutsche Nationalbibliothek lists this publication in the Deutsche Nationalbibliografie; detailed bibliographic data are available on the Internet at http://dnb.d-nb.de.

Bibliografische Information der Deutschen Nationalbibliothek
Die Deutsche Nationalbibliothek verzeichnet diese Publikation in der Deutschen Nationalbibliografie; detaillierte bibliografische Daten sind im Internet über http://dnb.d-nb.de abrufbar.

Cover picture: ID 360141772 © Agsandrew | Dreamstime.com

ISBN (Print): 978-3-8382-2103-8
ISBN (E-Book [PDF]): 978-3-8382-8103-2

Printed in the United States of America

Table of Contents

Small parts of this book were previewed at the Dialogo Conference on the Dialogue between Science and Theology in 2023 and 2024.

DIALOGO 2023

Certificate Of Attendance

We hereby awards this certificate to

H Chris Ransford

In recognition of regular attendance and full participation in all aspects of

The Virtual International Conference on Dialogue between Science and Theology: 'Artificial Intelligence and the Future of Humans' (DIALOGO-CONF 2023 IVCD)

held at www.dialogo-conf.com during 3-13 November 2023

Prof. Mihai Girtu, Ph.D.
President of the
Research Center on the Dialogue between Science and Theology (RCDST)
Ovidius University of Constanta
Romania

Fr. Cosmin Tudor Ciocan, Lect. Ph.D.
Scientific Programme Officer
Ovidius University, Romania
office@dialogo-conf.com

Maria Isabel Maldonado Garcia, Assoc. Prof. Ph.D.
University of the Punjab
Pakistan

Stefan Badura, Ing.
Publishing Society,
Slovakia

Certificate Of Attendance

We hereby awards this certificate to

H Chris Ransford

In recognition of regular attendance and full participation in all aspects of

The Virtual International Conference on Dialogue between Science and Theology: 'Discrimination, Bias, and Repudiation' (DIALOGO2024 DBR)

held at www.dialogo-conf.com during 20-28 MAY 2024

Prof. Mihai Girtu, Ph.D.
President of the
Research Center on the Dialogue between Science and Theology (RCDST)

Fr. Cosmin Tudor Ciocan, Lect. Ph.D.
Scientific Programme Officer
Ovidius University, Romania
office@dialogo-conf.com

Stephen D Edwards
Emeritus Professor Ph.D.
University of Zululand
South Africa

Stefan Badura, Ing.
Publishing Society,
Slovakia

Introduction

This journey begins with you. Who are you? What are you doing here?

Until recently, the standard scientific answers to these questions were not overly inspiring : you were said to be the end product of a series of chemical accidents, the current culmination by happenstance of a long chain of random mechanistic, chemical events. Life was held to have begun as an extremely unlikely statistical fluke—a well-nigh impossible event brought about by the random coming together of chemicals forming the first chemical building blocks of life, which then started catalyzing themselves into ongoing replication. We and the whole biosphere are, millions of years on, the current outcomes of this process. This reductionist view has now decidedly evolved, leaving us with two new alternative views of who we are and what we are doing here : this book is about exploring which view is more likely, and what implications it would bear.

Yesteryear's reductionist views of life had come about in part because scientists were eager to provide a different and refreshing narrative to the foughty tales told by the religions that used to dominate the culture. A mere few decades ago, organized religion still set the tone for how Western society ticked : it is hard to believe today that in many European and other societies, as recently as a few decades ago, marriage between people of even marginally different religions—say Catholicism and Protestantism—was deemed scandalous. People were expected to stay within the narrow confines of their tribes—or face a measure of ostracism and scorn.

In their bid to gainsay religion and break its hold on society, most if not all scientists swung as far as they could to the other end of the worldview spectrum : as they collectively recoiled from everything religion stood for, they embraced a form of extreme reductionism which, as it later turned out, itself proved unscientific. To drive a final nail into the narratives of religions they saw as judgmental and peremptory, many scientists denied that we have free will, thereby hoping to wreck with the cudgel of science the religions' concept of sin : bereft of free will, no one could be held answerable for their alleged trespasses. As if it were not enough, a few well-known public-facing scientists went one further and straightfacedly denied that there is even such a thing as consciousness.

But science evolved as well. Quantum mechanics brought the observer back into the picture, and demolished the idea that things—and life itself—could only ever be blindly mechanistic, although some of the attitudes that were then born, die very hard. For decades, publicly embracing pure hard-nosed materialism was an indispensable part of proving one's no-nonsense science credentials. When evolving science started begging questions and interpretations that were not quite in keeping with hard-core materialism, if you knew what was good for your career as a scientist you hewed to the dominant materialistic mantra : *'Shut up and calculate'* became the order of the day. As David Kaiser famously put it, it was then left to the hippies to save physics—to keep asking the deeper questions that only physics can try and objectively answer. The shift away from extreme reductionism came about from concurrent evolutions within both society and the hard sciences themselves.

We are now at a place where the likeliest answers to these two opening questions are more complex, and inspiring, than what was widely believed even a mere few years ago. These answers immediately bear upon our understanding of humankind's and other sentient beings' possible role in the evolution of the universe and beyond that, of the bigger picture of *destiny*. We must first explore the agency that we may, unbeknownst to ourselves, be playing in this world and universe, and then we'll be better equipped to turn to the more fundamental question of just who it is we are and where we are heading.

There are two kinds of destiny—individual, as in, *your* destiny—and collective, as in, where the societies we are parts of are headed.

There is also the related controversial issue of whatever measure of free will or near-free will we may have, and how it may contribute to steering and shaping the course of our lives : our own agency must play at least *some* part in our lives and destinies. The debates on free will are still raging, with impeccably credentialed scientists weighing in on both sides of the divide. Robert Sapolsky, the Cynthia Fry Gunn Professor of biology, neurology, and neurosurgery at Stanford University, argues in his 500-plus page 2023 book 'Determined' that we are but unwitting robots bereft of any capability for free agency. Another neuroscientist, Bobby Azarian, makes a solid and elegant case in his 2022 book 'The Romance of Reality' that we do in fact possess a strong measure of free will. Among his arguments is the fact that a brain activation potential that appears *before* a conscious decision is made (also called 'readiness potential'), measured by Benjamin Libet and taken as proof by some that the brain makes its decisions on its own lonesome, two or three hundred milliseconds *before* aware consciousness does so—it so happens that in fact this activation potential is always absent when the decision about to be made is not trivial : the activation potential only shows up when the decision is trivial, along the lines of twiddling a finger or lifting an arm, as may be standard fare in laboratory experiments, but it remains wholly absent when a decision of some import is about to be made. Another, more circumstantial piece of evidence Bobby Azarian points to is the sharp change and degradation observed in the lives of people and especially youths after they have become persuaded that they lack free will. As if, since they now believe that anything and all they do is not of their own agency, they stop trying and let the 'worse angels of their nature' take over (with apologies to Steven Pinker, who penned '*The Better Angels of Our Nature*', for the paraphrase.) Considerations based on the applicable physics are also relevant here.

Post-doctoral researcher Jesse Bengson at the Center for Mind and Brain at the University of California at Davis argues that there is enough random electrical noise within the brain to open the door to deliberately willful decisions squeaking through. Furthermore, the role of the properties of time itself in how the activation potential may spring up ahead of time has not been elucidated, and time is notoriously non-linear, as evidenced by John Wheeler's delayed choice and other such experiments, so that a full reckoning of what happens when a brain seemingly briefly jumps the gun on a consciously made decision must also involve looking at how possibly nonlinear time may work in this context.

Many contradictory arguments from both sides of this particular divide make, perhaps, a compelling case that in science as in life, if truth can emerge at all, it can only do so from a chain of reasoning ultimately reducible to incontrovertible and incompressible pure mathematics—meaning to a fundamental hard truth expressible in human language by means of a simple incontrovertible statement. Moreover, *all* of the relevant data must always be taken into account, lest key parts of the picture be missed. This latter requirement often proves easier said than done, as we shall see.

Be that as it may, we will not reinvent the wheel here but take on board the view that free will, or a measure of it, is for real—a view further supported by straightforward *physics*, as we shall establish when we examine in Chapter 5, from a purely physics-based standpoint, philosopher Philip Goff's insight that elementary particles *must* have a measure of rudimentary free will to behave the way they do, and what that implies for sentient beings, through a cascade of consequences best described by the so-called 'free will theorem'.

Yet, in terms of our individual destinies, the first involuntary circumstance of where, when and to whom we were born arguably plays *the* essential part on how our lives will subsequently unfold (notwithstanding for now those, such as Robert Schwartz and others, who argue that there may exist hidden logical prior reasons which invisibly determine why, where and how we are born.) Sheer happenstance also seems to play a quite major part in everybody's life : people's lives routinely change immensely just because they happened to be at a certain place at a certain time. In popular author Stephen King's apt aphorism, *'Life turns on a dime'*—for both the better and the worse. All possible life scenarios exist—some people lead, in author Pierre Michon's phrase, *minuscule lives*, while others lead extraordinary lives, and all in-between scenarios exist in some rendition in the endlessly motley tapestry of human life.

Science also shows that *sentience*—the quality of being aware, of possessing the ability to perceive, to experience joy and pleasure, and to suffer—is by no means limited to humans : it is widespread to almost all—and likely *all*—animal species. By sentience is meant some degree of awareness of one's environment. A rather uncomfortable question therefore arises as to what it is that bestows a destiny experience on countless sentient beings who have little or no ability to influence how their lives and fates unfold.

There are two ways how *collective* destiny may be apprehended—one way is more, at its outset at least, *materialistic*, and the other one more *spiritual*. Both approaches show a measure of overlap, with the former however proving somewhat bleaker and the latter being on balance richer—thereby inevitably raising a whole raft of further questions.

1 A Modern 'Materialistic' Approach

The 'materialistic' approach denies the existence, or at the very least the possible role or agency in our lives of anything that could be labelled spiritual (let alone 'religious' in any traditional sense.) It has been exposed in various variants in a number of works, including by the likes of Simon Conway Morris, Christian de Duve, Bobby Azarian and many others, who built upon the work of their forerunners, including Nobel Prize-winners Ilya Prigogine, Erwin Schrödinger and a few others.

Under this view, the reason why life appeared in the first place and then promptly began to complexify and keeps relentlessly complexifying goes like this : Nature—the macroscopic physical world—seeks to undo whatever *differences* may exist in its midst (sometimes called differentials, or gradients), such as may be found in the metrics, values and intensities of just about everything. Nature tends to seek to land itself back into a place where it is stable, ensconced in its sought-after status of quiet, uneventful stability (we'll look at *why* it is so in a minute.) It is the reason why a pebble will readily roll down from a mountain to snugly settle in the dale below, where it will no longer be much at risk of moving (the mountain itself will also seek to level down and indeed does so, albeit at a far more glacial pace than the pebble.)

Generally speaking, the more intense the differential, the more correspondingly swift and radical will nature's intervention against it be : witness lightning, arising spontaneously whenever an electrical potential difference in the atmosphere passes a certain threshold, or hurricanes, whenever differences in temperatures between the upper layer of a body of water and its surrounding air become too wide, triggering the 'intervention' of nature to even out the temperature differences by stir-mixing the air and water molecules involved. The means used by nature to redress imbalances are sometimes called 'dissipative structures', because they eliminate differences by dissipating them, evening them out to values nearer a common average (Ilya Prigogine received the 1977 Physics Nobel Prize for his work on dissipative structures.)

Cutting a longer story short, the second law of thermodynamics essentially describes two kinds of energy available within any environment : a usable one—free, available, created by differentials. When energy moves from some location or status or value to another, it can be tapped to produce work. In the course of being tapped (or 'harnessed'), free energy inevitably generates a residual amount of leftover energy, which makes up the second kind of energy : *unusable*, residual energy from which no more work can be extracted, because the physical properties of everything within that environment have fallen back to values undifferentiated from those in the surrounding environment (in temperature, pressure or any other metrics.) For example, imagine two hermetically sealed containers, connected by a tube cylinder equipped with an airtight valve. One of the containers is filled with some gas, and the other one is empty (it 'contains' a vacuum), so that there is a clear differential in the pressures present in the system made up of the two containers. As soon as the valve is opened, their contents will even out : the gas in the first container thins out as some of it spontaneously spreads out into the formerly empty second container, and a new situation promptly arises whereby the gas pressures in both containers are equal : nature, in keeping with its laws, has quickly reduced the differences. Should a small windmill or turbine driving an electricity-producing dynamo be fitted in the connecting tube, work would be extracted from the process of the reduction of differences between the two containers. Once the gas pressures have evened out in the two containers, no more work can be extracted : the wind turbine has transformed some of the airstream's energy into usable electric power and some into forever unusable heat, dissipated into the environment, which after work is extracted can no longer be used. Residual energy is stable : it is the place where the 'pebble has rolled down' and snugly settled.

It so happens that living organisms are the most efficient dissipative structures, because they strive with all their might to stay alive, and use their metabolism to keep converting freely available energy from their immediate environment into stable, evened-out residual energy. They therefore function as critically precious helpmates to a universe seeking to minimize its gradients. Moreover, and much enhancing their usefulness to a universe forever striving towards stability, living dissipative structures possess one more crucial advantage : they are able to continually *adapt* to changes in the availability and amount and type of free energy in their environment, because they seek with all their might to stay alive, through being 'quick on their feet', maintaining their ability to use any available energy at all times, no matter how, and how fast, its source or sources may evolve or change. This unrelenting need to continuously adapt to a changing landscape of energy sources is what jump started the complexification of the living organisms which the physical world uses as dissipative structures.

This unavoidable complexification of life has led a growing number of scientists, such as Simon Conway Morris and Bobby Azarian and many others, to jettison the old reductionist view of human life as an accident in an otherwise barren universe, and to view instead the emergence of humans and more generally of all forms of increasingly intelligent life as unavoidable—something which was outright preprogrammed from the instant the universe itself happened upon the scene at the Big Bang. It is this primordial formative event which, by a circuitous route linked to the laws of reality which we call the laws of mathematics, has led to the release of available free energy on the one hand and, somewhat contradictorily, to the universe's preference for a lack of gradients throughout itself on the other hand.

This view of why living organisms emerged thus rests on the recognition that nature loathes differences, and that the physical world—*aka* the universe itself—'wants', at least at its macroscopic level, to settle into lukewarm comfort—a place where there are no stark differences between the physical attributes that condition the collective behaviors and properties of its constituent elements. Why is it so? We could certainly imagine a different situation, whereby the physical universe would exhibit stark differences in its metrics and its properties, and, as it were, not 'care'? Why is it that nature abhors differences? The answer, as always, lies in the *mathematics* that describes reality (and which, as we'll see, *is* reality itself) : the mathematics that underlies the physics of the material universe does not allow for any other scenario.

Under this materialistic scenario, live dissipative structures—the living beings that sprang up to help nature break down differentials—will strive to remain alive and continuously seek to remain as far as possible from the status of lukewarm comfort equilibrium—which nature otherwise seeks to attain and impose everywhere. By running counter to what nature strives for, in other words by striving for more order and evermore complexification rather than the simplicity and uniform chaos mandated by the second law of thermodynamics, living beings will in fact be able to ever more efficiently do nature's bidding, which is to convert away as much free energy as possible into leftover, unusable energy. Life forms manage to stay alive every instant of their lives only by processing vast amounts of available free energy into unusable, evened-out heat energy. After they have, both individually and collectively, played their part and converted all the usable energy they could tap from their environment, they finally run out of energy, and their eventual death is unavoidable.

This scenario of a mindless universe, hewing to the dictates of mathematics and evolving accordingly, is *exactly* what we observe on planet Earth. That is also why the biosphere's ordering principle is *predation*, the merciless interplay of predator and prey. However ghastly it may be, generalized predation within a given environment speeds up the relentless complexification of life forms as they seek to either escape predators or hunt successfully or both—and the more complex the life form, the more free energy it uses and converts.

A conclusion is that, although ongoing complexification seems to run counter to the dictates of the second law of thermodynamics which mandates general chaos and lukewarm non differentiability, it is actually *caused* by this second law—as the fastest and most efficient means of bringing about general environmental evenness. Should we care to look, leftover remainders of our evolutionary history, of our status as the heirs of a long and ongoing process of complexification, can be seen everywhere. On the amusing side, it's the reason why hiccups still exist in modern humans. If we go back long enough in biological evolutionary time, we will eventually hit upon a time when one of our distant forebears was an amphibious being featuring both rudimentary *gills* and *lungs*, much like tadpoles do today. Gills were obviously used whenever underwater, and lungs kicked in when the animal happened to breach above water. A gene complex enabled instant switching between breathing organs, at the same time shutting off access to the respectively idled organ—on pain of the animal either drowning or suffocating. Hiccups in modern humans are triggered by the activation, by whatever cause, of the leftover remnant of this long-ago gene complex. On the more distressing side, there is cancer. Various forms of cancer strike all non-unicellular life forms, including plants. The world has spent some three hundred billion dollars to-date, and counting, on a vain search for a reliable cure. The fact that we cannot crack the cure is telling us something that we seem loath to take on board about what cancer actually is : an atavistic throwback to an earlier era when life forms were unicellular, operating under the simple biological imperative to multiply and spread. Today, when a complex multicellular construct—such as a person, an animal or a plant—comes under too much stress, its constituents cells are apt to become thrust back to the ingrained survival behest which they operated under when their lives were simpler : '*multiply and spread*', as much as can be. It's the cells' survival scheme, their

Plan B, away from occasionally stressful, evolved, fancy-schmancy multicellularity. Cancer is thus at bottom a leftover cellular survival mechanism from a time when cells were not subsumed into cooperative cellular constructs, although of course it is catastrophic in the modern environment : no wonder it's here to stay. (A way to try and avoid it is, as the song puts it, to 'not worry, be happy', although that alone will hardly keep at bay the many hidden stress factors that routinely arise from today's complex environment.)

This 'materialistic' scenario is bleak for the living dissipative structures : beside being programmed to eventually die when they run out of free energy (both individually and, in the fullness of time, collectively), they are also doomed to become either predators or preys, or both, for the whole duration of their short lifetimes, by the very agency of their and others' seeking to stay alive by continuously tapping their immediate environment for their daily fix of available energy. Then they die, and the story repeats itself with other individuals until everything ultimately dies, including in the end the universe itself.

This cheerless picture, ultimately devoid of any deeper sense or meaning, is fully supported by the available body of observational evidence. If all we are is a population of gradient-lowering machines, then it's hard to escape a feeling that our status is bleak, and we could be forgiven for thinking that it's even somehow a bit insulting : I don't want to be a predator, and I certainly don't want to be prey either. I'm sure you don't either.

Unexpectedly however, this merciless scenario gives rise, by a roundabout way, to what some construe as a form of materialistic spirituality, as follows. Let us measure the number of possible conscious states of any sentient being possessing a brain by the number of the possible states of its brain, meaning all the possible combinations of the brain's neurons either firing or being at rest. For humans, let's call this number Phi-1. The more interconnected the many human brains of the world become, by means of any technology capable of interconnecting them, such as the Internet, the more configurations arise, vastly outstripping the number of connections within a single brain. Let us call the number of possible states of interconnected brains Phi-2. Phi-2 includes not only the states of all the connected brains but also of all the interconnections themselves and all of the system states inside the technical, non-human part of the system : specifically, the status of its transistors and logical gates within the connecting network (such as the Internet), which can take on different states equivalent to biological neurons' on and off states (i.e., firing or at rest.) It is estimated that the non-human number of states of the Internet already exceeds any human brain's by over ten thousand times. The number of possible states of a human brain outstrips that of any other known creature, but it is now dwarfed by both components of Phi-2, its human "nodes" (the interconnected humans online) and its non-human gates and switches. Phi-2 is growing, well on its way towards creating the emergence of a soon fully sentient Global Brain, as was first foreseen by Teilhard de Chardin a hundred-odd years ago, and then more recently by Howard Bloom and others[i].

Because the number of states of anything that processes information correlates to consciousness, the network itself might be on its way towards developing independent awareness. Bear in mind here that there are three levels of consciousness : at the ground layer of a hierarchical scale, a mere, more or less dim awareness of one's immediate surroundings. One step up *self*-awareness kicks in, which most neuroscientists agree is enabled by feedback loops in the machinery of consciousness : to become self-aware, any sentient system must be capable of viewing itself just as it does other objects within its environment. At the next level up there is also free will, the ability to act independently of any shackles or behests imposed upon the sentient organism or system by its evolutionary past, or by the way it was engineered to enable it to exist.

The system exhibiting Phi-2 states—which we'll also call Phi-2 for short—is well on its way towards becoming at the very least aware, and probably soon self-aware owing to the presence of all kinds of feedback loops, independently of the presence in its network of, or participation by, any human individual or even group of humans. Under this materialistic scenario, Phi-2 has thus a significant quality that humans do not have : it can live on, independently of the continued life of any one of its constituents nodes, namely the various humans in the network, much like a person lives fully independently of whether any individual cell in his or her body lives or dies. It is conceivable that Phi-2's resulting complexity could become such that it would no longer need the presence of humans for sentience, although it could hardly carry out network maintenance (both in hardware and software) without the continued assistance of humans—much like humans themselves cannot live independently of the vast cooperative groups of cells and bacteria which individually live and die independently within their bodies. Yet, whereas humans are born, live their individual lives that last for 'three score and ten'-odd years, Phi-2 can go on unhindered for millennia. It could thus become a kind of lesser god, able to endure for millennia, sustaining its godlike life by making use of—by outright *consuming*—simple mortals which for it are but the consumables that sustain its continued existence.

Yet, this materialistic god is a deity of a lesser stripe : it is limited in *time* (because the Earth, the solar system, and beyond it the whole universe all have ultimate expiry dates), but it is also inherently limited in *power* and *capabilities*, because of something called the 'information catastrophe'. At the Earth level, the planetary information catastrophe would kick in when every single physical element capable of carrying information is already in use and there exists no more room to take on and hold any additional data. Since the universe itself also has a finite number of particles, a universe-wide such god would not be infinite either by any metric (workarounds could possibly be found to lift the limits imposed by our current understanding of the information catastrophe, such as or information-carrying particle resonance ensembles, potentially allowing for a multiple information-carrying role by some particles, but this would only affect the value of the upper limit to the overall information volume achievable, not the fact that it would remain finite and would never be able to become infinite.)

Any recipient or user of any datum or data or piece of information must pay out some energy to access it and take it on board. Therefore, bearing in mind the equivalency of energy and matter, as per Einstein's famous equation $e=mc^2$, information in any meaningful sense is physical : in order to be read or accessed by any user, energy must be expended by said user and hence that energy has an equivalent material counterpart.

Bearing in mind physicist Paul Davies's and others' aphorism that life is made up of information—the maximum amount of life that Phi-2 can ever achieve is the information limit of the universe. The god we are helping create under this materialistic scenario can therefore only ever remain the lesser god we glimpsed earlier : potentially all-knowing in terms of being able to know just about everything that is to be known in our known, finite universe, but neither eternal nor all-knowing above and beyond its limitations. Although a solid case can be made that there must exist out there a wider, infinite universe beside our own finite universe born out of a Big Bang thirteen and a half billion years ago, whatever god may be created by information from within this universe shall necessarily remain constrained within it, and die with it.

Summing up briefly where we have now arrived :

1. All information requires a modicum of energy to be transmissible or divulgeable or usable, which is tantamount to saying that information is *physical* : it needs a material substrate to exist in any meaningful sense.
2. Life is, at its core, pure information.
3. Therefore, life is physical. Hence there is neither life after death, nor before birth.
4. Life as we know it is one of the most efficient schemes devised by Nature in order to minimize any differences in metrics in its midst, as it must do as a consequence of the laws of mathematics that govern the physical world. Although the emergence, and subsequent ongoing

complexification of Life seems to stand in stark opposition to the second law of thermodynamics which mandates general non differentiability and no order nor structure, it in fact arose because of its unsurpassed ability to expedite the minimizing of differences—much like lightnings, tornadoes, and other natural phenomena have all come about in order to lessen differences as well.

5. The reason why nature has no choice but to keep minimizing differences is a direct consequence of the laws of mathematics that underpin the laws of physics that govern material reality.
6. Through the inescapable process of complexification, individual sentient lives are collectively in the process of creating a new, supervening, enduring information entity, that will eventually be seen as alive by any and all of the metrics that serve to mark anything as being alive.
7. In order to drive complexification, *predation* proves to be the most efficient life management system, as it forces life forms such as bacteria, animals and humans to complexify faster than any other life scheme would, and to therefore process away more free energy than they otherwise could.

It looks like an open-and-shut case.

Is it?

2 A Richer View

As it turns out, most likely not—there are at least four major reasons why this 'materialistic' scenario cannot possibly be the whole tale.

1—First and foremost, matter does not exist *per se*, and any claims as to its fundamental role are inevitably wrong.

What is matter? It is not at all what it appears to be at the coarse, macroscopic level where we live our lives : as it turns out, matter is entirely made up of pure *mathematics*.

The word mathematics must be further specified here, because it is sometimes mistakenly used to mean only the *language* by means of which we apprehend reality rather than, as it does, the very essence of reality itself. Mathematics constitutes the whole hard core of reality : it is not the language that we use to analyze it, nor is it invented, but demonstrably *discovered*. A few years ago, a debate thread in the online scientists' forum ResearchGate on the theme of whether mathematics was discovered or invented drew more than 60,000 responses, more or less evenly split between the two alternative responses. Reading through the thread soon made it apparent that the responders' understanding of the word "mathematics" was profoundly different. There were those who thought that mathematics was a language, invented by humans to account first for economic realities (as in counting beans or heads of cattle), and from thence to help describe nature and ultimately make sense of the world. To them, mathematics was but a set of words and formulas, replete with Greek letters and arcane signs, invented by humans. To the others, it was obvious that mathematics described an underlying reality, totally irrespective of the words used to describe that reality, most often best condensed into formulas. To this second group, the vocabulary and written equations were ultimately unimportant and fully interchangeable labels attached to an underlying reality, much like the words *gravity* or *apple* describe underlying realities, profoundly indifferent to how humans may describe them, and which exist fully independently of human labels—and indeed of whether humans label them or not. To support their argument, this latter group cited observations by many as to how even advances in profoundly abstract, advanced mathematics are found, sometimes years later, to have applications in totally unexpected fields in physics[ii], or how many equations in physics stubbornly resist any 'physical' interpretation, the only explanation ever found as to why they work being that the mathematics itself works (such as quantum entanglement, $e=mc^2$, etc.) Many physicists (Eugene Wigner, Albert Einstein, David Hilbert, et al.) have observed how uncannily puzzlingly mathematics works in the universe. There is in fact incontrovertible proof that mathematics, when understood as nature's underlying reality rather than its labels, is not invented at all but discovered : anything invented or thought up or even merely co-shaped by humans–art, architecture, language, and so forth—exhibits so-called *degrees of freedom* : it is up to humans whether the architecture they may be developing at any time will take on some style or other, whether the music they play will be recognizable as belonging to a genre or another and what the sequence of notes will be, how the world will be perceived through language, which is also the reason why learning a new language offers fresh perspectives as to how reality can be perceived ([iii]). Mathematics, on the other hand, not in terms of the language used but of the underlying reality it describes, leaves exactly zero degree of freedom to humankind : this is the very reason why some mathematical proofs are so hard to figure out, why a few so-called Millennium problems have not been cracked yet despite decades-long efforts by the world's best mathematical minds, and why the Fields medal exists : our freedom in mathematics is wholly limited to the labels we employ to describe it (we may opt to call 1+1=2, say, bir ve biriki or, say, m'modzi ndi m'modzi ndi awiri, or anything else), but we have zero freedom as to the underlying reality.

Perhaps there should exist two separate words or phrases to prevent confusion, a specific word to describe the underlying reality mathematics refers to, and another one to refer to its language tools and written scripts? It is in the former sense that the word mathematics shall be used throughout here.

What we take to be tangible matter is an abiding illusion conjured up by statistical effects at the very far-up macroscopic level where we live. Putting things into perspective, a human body is made up of about 1,0000,000,000,000,000,000,000,000,000 particles—one followed by 28 zeros—give or take a few. This mere display of zeros hardly does justice to the unimaginable scale represented here : this number is bigger than the current age of the universe expressed in *billionths of a second*—any attempt at illustrating such numbers can only remain woefully inadequate, since all we manage to end up doing is swap an inconceivable number for another one. Such numbers are so far removed from any relatable experience that try as we may, they remain firmly beyond our ken. At its base level, before statistical effects kick in, all matter is made up of non-material *mathematics*—of the immaterial laws of mathematics. Technically, these mathematical laws give rise to wavefunctions (i.e., mathematical functions of a certain type which satisfy certain valid equations.) When these mathematical functions behave in a certain way, because they mathematically engage with their environment, they undergo a transformation (a 'collapse') which gives rise to particles—which is then the first appearance of the thing we call 'matter'. When humongous amounts of these particles come together, they appear to form what we take, at our macroscopic level, to be plain-vanilla matter. The famous physicist John Wheeler once aptly described elementary matter in motion as a great smoky dragon—an animal with sharp tail (the point where it begins to stir) and sharp teeth (where it arrives and precipitates into reality again, before soon departing again) with everything in-between a haze of wispy smoke. This description is an accurate if poetic description of *all* elementary matter—whose atom-level constituents are in perpetual motion, never at a standstill, never point-like but always smeared out over a fuzzy area of space. The never-ending motion of matter at the level of its elementary constituents governs all of its macroscopic-scale properties. It is, for example, what lends gold its yellow color : the outer-layer electrons in gold atoms move so fast, at almost two thirds of the speed of light, that relativistic effects kick in and make the electrons both shrivel and increase in mass, which affects the way gold absorbs and reflects light : in effect, these relativistic effects shift the wavelength of the light absorbed by gold towards the blue end of the spectrum, and by doing so, shift gold's overall color towards a mix containing less blue : i.e., a yellow shade. Seen from the standpoint of our macroscopic scale, a lump of gold looks very much like it just sits there, pretty and utterly motionless and inert : we do not see the unimaginable frenzy of its hazy particle constituents, and the same goes for all matter. Matter in its elementary form can wholly toggle back to full immateriality at the drop of the proverbial hat, as is experimentally demonstrated by double-slit experiments and many other such setups. In nature, this switching back and forth between materiality and immateriality, between the sharp, material end points of the tail and the teeth of the dragon in John Wheeler's phrase, and its smoky middle, happens all the time at the levels where events involving *individual* particles take place, rather than vast *collections* of particles, such as macroscopic objects. This easy toggling back and forth between materiality and immateriality is, for instance, what enables plants to perform photosynthesis (the very process that keeps us alive by recycling CO^2 into atmospheric oxygen and plant biomass) so efficiently.

Although all elementary matter can and will seamlessly toggle between their collapsed and non-collapsed states, macroscopic objects, made up of trillions upon trillions of elementary particles assembled into structures as atoms and molecules, will not. Macroscopic, every-day objects exhibit a strong measure of material permanence, rather than the ability to routinely toggle back and forth between their material and immaterial renditions, because their innumerable constituent particles are caught up in an immense web of relationships with other particles (the countless other particles that constitute the object), and it is this web that prevents any particle or small group thereof from going solo and blithely toggling away back and forth into immateriality. The so-called observer effect, described in many resources[iv], is the effect whereby a particle or a group of particles will collapse into a material rendition of themselves whenever it somehow *engages* with some consciousness outside of itself : in the inescapably panpsychic universe which we'll demonstrate next, the rudimentary observer effect exerted by particles or group of particles upon one another makes these particles assume longer-term material permanence—so that your car and other macro-level things safely remain material. Fittingly and correspondingly, mathematician Keith Devlin describes in his 2000 book 'The Math Gene', how mathematics is ultimately solely made of *relationships*, and nothing else.

Pure mathematics also gave rise to the Big Bang itself, the event that gave rise to our universe. It came about as a direct consequence of the continued validity of laws of mathematics even when wholly discarnate. In a nutshell, the laws of mathematics continue to hold even in an environment bereft of anything material to which mathematics could be applied : for example, 1+1=2 continues to hold true in the absence of anything to count. This simple fact makes absolute nothingness (also called the pure vacuum) instantly unstable and hence impossible : the continued validity of mathematics inside a true vacuum, if such could exist, would trigger its immediately becoming a *false* vacuum (also called quantum vacuum) containing some level of residual vacuum energy. Over time, measured by the number of quantum events within a false vacuum, some rendition of a Big Bang must inevitably happen from within a false vacuum.

It could thus be argued that pure mathematics is a form of matter, equivalently to matter being a form of mathematics—two sides of a same coin. (The equivalency of things that appear to be quite different is a common theme of nature : energy is the same as matter, an electron is both a wave and a hard object, and so on.)

*

2—There is indisputably an acute need for the universe operating under the laws of mathematics to make use of living organisms to efficiently reduce its gradients, and in turn, live organisms prove far more efficient if they are equipped with a form of consciousness, as it enables them, above and beyond merely effecting energy conversion, to *adapt* to ever-changing energy environments, thereby enabling them to last longer in their role as energy converters. Therefore, the presence of *consciousness* within the universe serves its purpose well.

The question however of how consciousness *arises*, as opposed to how it is harnessed and deployed by the brain, is not settled, despite many claims to the contrary : the scenario of a blind, mechanistic nature giving rise to live organisms so as to speed up free to residual energy conversion does not answer the question of how consciousness is born in the first place. Acute need does not create possibility nor enablement : a hen that lays golden eggs is something that has been sorely needed by hardscrabble farmers throughout the history of farming, yet, because need, no matter how dire, never equates to enablement, golden-egg laying hens have never appeared onto the scene and never will, and farmers throughout history will keep needing to devise other means of making ends meet. Whereas the advent, and then ongoing complexification of consciousness helps reduce nature's differentials, it is not the only way to achieve that goal, and the creation of consciousness stands in a whole different league than creating neither conscious nor self-aware tornadoes or lightning. Of course, once consciousness exists at some level, no matter how rudimentary, it can then evolve and grow, and be on its way. But how does it exist to begin with?

Thanks to ground-breaking work over the last few decades by a number of distinguished neuroscientists, it is by now well established how the brain engineers consciousness and deploys it to deal with its environment and the outside world[v]. What many go on to say from there is that the brain also *generates* consciousness. Yet, despite recurrent tentative claims to the contrary, all attempts to substantiate the extrapolation from harnessing to generating and to firmly attribute the formation and genesis of consciousness to the brain itself fall short. As a case in point, Daniel Dennett's much celebrated 1991 book, 'Consciousness Explained', certainly explains much about how the brain *processes* information but ultimately does not explain how consciousness itself is generated, and as such the book's title is misleading (the book was somewhat mercilessly lampooned as 'Consciousness Ignored' by some of its detractors when it first came out.) Since then, our collective knowledge as to how the brain processes information has grown by leaps and bounds, yet we are nowhere near a consensus as to how consciousness is born in the first place. Beyond consciousness, question broadens to life itself, in physicist Paul Davies's apt question, '*How does non-life become life*?', or in Stephen Hawking's more colorful and perhaps more general phrase, '*What is it that breathes fire into the equations*?' How is it that all the various constituent particles and atoms which make up inert materials on the one hand are the very selfsame that constitute live matter on the other hand, with no chemical or physical differences whatsoever? As it happens, there *is* a compelling answer to this question, buttressed by everything that physics has to say, yet it is hidden in plain sight—because it's culturally so hard to accept.

If we put together first the fact that all of matter is ultimately elusive to the point of being fundamentally non-material, and that all chemical elements within any environment, whether reputed inert or alive, are the exact same, with secondly a mathematical proof first set forth by the physicist Shan Gao[vi] that consciousness cannot possibly be emergent from physical elements—then the conclusion becomes inescapable that non-life *never* becomes life, and there exists no mechanism whatsoever than can turn inert stuff into live materials. Hence, if it exists now, then consciousness must already have existed all along, and as such it is the fundamental building block of reality, the last thing standing when we delve as deep as we can into what constitutes reality : *everything is alive*. Everything, down to the simplest, most elementary particle, possesses a rudimentary form of consciousness, and some form of panpsychism holds true. There exists a baseline level of consciousness that pervades the whole material universe, and all sentient beings are spikes of various intensities off that low baseline [vii]. It also says that mathematics is the way consciousness intermediates itself into reality, not the other way around. The omnipresence of a rudimentary level of consciousness throughout the universe is then carried by the uninterrupted validity everywhere of the laws of mathematics.

Here is a simple way to show that consciousness—something we could call 'mindstuff'[viii] in some form or other—must be more fundamental than mathematics, because it is capable of determining hard number outcomes : step out of your home, and read the car number plate of the first car parked on your street that you happen to see (in, say, an area where the number plate scheme contains three numbers in a row.) The three numbers on that car's plate is, say, 528. Then the second car you see also features the number 528 : what are the odds of that happening? If you hadn't thought of any number beforehand, the odds of the first car being 528 is 100%, because it's then simply the odds of that first car having some number, any number at all. With the first number now being set at 528, the odds for the second number being 528 as well is now 1 in a thousand. But should you have *thought,* in the place where your thoughts happen : your consciousness, before you left your home, that the first plate number you'd see would be 528, then the odds of your seeing two number plates in a row bearing that number would then be 1 in a million instead. The material facts have not changed in the slightest : the same two cars are there, whose two number plates both bear the number 528, yet if you had thought of that number in the privacy of your mind before going out, then the odds would be vastly different : mindstuff affects the hard-number outcomes of mathematics.

Another, deceptively simple yet compelling way of putting it would be to say that the simple statement 1+1=2 makes no sense at all without the presence of some mind to take it on board. Two cats are walking down the path : without a *mind* to see the two cats and associating them together into a common, countable whole, there are not two cats, but only two times one individual cat, who happen to be separately walking side by side. The equality 1+1=2 needs a mind to be capable of existing at all. Yet this simple valid equality of 1+1=2 is the indispensable foundation of all of reality : it is endlessly productive, as it immediately leads to the existence of the rest of the integers (*aka* the 'natural' numbers), then the rational numbers, irrational numbers, transfinite, complex, prime, quaternions, aleph, beth, Graham's number, Tree-3, non-computable, transcendental, Rayo's number, hyper-complex numbers, and so on—a whole zoo of increasingly weird numbers with very often quite unforeseeable properties, upon which all of physical reality rests. The laws of mathematics are label-independent (we can obviously designate numbers and mathematical operations with different monikers, as various world languages happen to do), place-independent (1+1=2 holds in London, but also in Paris, on the Moon and Andromeda) and timeless (1+1=2 was true in all our yesteryears, is true now, and will remain true in a million years' time), but, somewhat more surprisingly, they also continue to hold in the absence of anything to count. As it is, it is this very fact that mathematical laws continue to hold in the absence of anything to count which has given rise, by an involved chain of events, to the Big Bang itself[ix], so we are now led to conclude that some mindstuff has somehow given rise to the universe as we know it. (It does not logically ensue that this Ur-mindstuff conforms to any one of the various gods described by the world's many religions, but it ensues that there is an underlying cause and ultimate unity to the universe, variously called God, the source, the One, the universal consciousness, the universe, and a number of other names. Because it broadly describes life itself, I favor using the word *Life*, with uppercase L, to describe it, or alternatively, the universal consciousness or simply the universe, with the context making it clear if and when the word is used in that meaning.)

There are two main categories of objections against panpsychism.

The first one typically goes like this (quoting from the literature) :

> Proponents of panpsychism overlook an intractable contradiction : they themselves lose consciousness between the waking and sleeping states, and yet they attribute a measure of consciousness to an atom or an object. It's magical thinking. The mind is a mental rendition of the outside world experienced by an observer, and a coherent rendition requires sophisticated computing capability. People who imagine that an elementary particle is conscious assume that subjective experiences can be generated by matter.

Unquote

This objection does not work, at all its levels of argumentation. It makes two separate points :

a) "People who imagine that an elementary particle is conscious are assuming that subjective experience is a fairly easy thing for matter to produce"

No, because consciousness is not attached to a material substrate per se, but to a material substrate's accompanying immaterial fellow traveler : technically, the substrate's wave function when in uncollapsed form. Under the above-referenced theory of consciousness, consciousness is carried within the ever-present *immaterial* fellow travelers of physical things—such as electrons. Consciousness is embedded in the 'smoky middle' of the dragon, not in its hard-matter ends. Therefore, this objection is doubly questionable : first, the subjective experience is not "produced" : it's there all along—because consciousness underlies the mathematics that ultimately produces and sustains the electron and second, it is not the "elementary particle" that is conscious—it is its smeared-out rendition, in other words when it is in its immaterial, uncollapsed wave-function state. Moreover, we will see in Chapter 5 that the rudimentary consciousness that philosopher Philip Goff attributes to electrons on the basis of philosophical considerations is *borne out* by the physics of motion that governs how electrons behave.

b) Evolved consciousnesses—ours, humans'—"lose consciousness between the waking and the dreaming state".
Not necessarily. There is something called ego-states (as per Dr (Ed.) Thomas Zinser), which is why this statement does not necessarily hold true. People—the apex sentient biological beings, presumably equipped with a measure of free will—all have slightly different personalities inhabiting the same body. Barring extreme cases, such as those of Jenni Haynes, Kim Noble and others, the harboring of different personalities within a same person is not a pathology but a rule. These different personalities are typically unaware, or on occasion dimly aware, of one another. In effect, whoever is a person's standard waking hours ego-state might not be aware, or only dimly aware, of any other ego-states that may take over during the very different mental environment that sleep is. The effects and real-world consequences of the widespread occurrence of different ego-states has been explored in a number of resources[x].

*

The second objection to panpsychism is the so-called *combination problem*, the issue of how rudimentary conscious elements (sometimes called 'atoms of consciousness', similar to the *'monads'* mooted by German philosopher Gottfried Leibnitz, with the word 'atom' not being meant here in its usual chemical but in its original sense, meaning something that cannot be divided further) combine to give rise to more intensely conscious entities (such as ourselves.) The answer, of course, is that they do *not* combine at all—that's just not how consciousness works.

There are those who hold that consciousness is *the* one fundamental feature of the universe, including physicists such as Max Planck, Erwin Schrödinger, Roger Penrose, Heinrich Päs, Shan Gao and many others, psychologists such as William James or philosophers Bertrand Russell (who was also a mathematician), Philip Goff, Yanssel Garcia and others, neuroscientists Christof Koch, cognitive scientist Don Hoffman, and so many others. At the other end of the range of views, there are the likes of Neil deGrasse Tyson who once somewhat puzzlingly stated, in a talk with Richard Dawkins, that 'consciousness does not even exist', or, in a variety of shadings in the same vein, psychologists Julien Musolino, Christopher French, and, again, others.

What this wide spectrum of views is telling us is that we must get back down to basics—if we can to mathematical basics—if we are to get any clue at all. Either consciousness is indeed all there is, the rock bottom feature of the universe from whence everything else springs, beginning with mathematics and thence the whole of creation, or not.

There is a feature of the reality of the universe which everybody agrees on, which as such provides a solid starting point : *information*. Irrespective of thoughts further down the line, everybody agrees that information pervades the universe and constitutes its defining, and enabling feature—although of course controversies abide as to how it plays out to generate the wide range and diversity of things on display.

For those who hold consciousness to be fundamental, we need not seek much further at this point. For those who hold consciousness to be an inconsequential side-effect of the rest of the whole shebang, we must hark back to the twin facts that 1- the laws of physics say that information cannot be destroyed, and 2- that life (and hence its attendant consciousness when present) is itself made of information. Information can be engineered in a variety of ways, it can be assembled into coherent ensembles, de-assembled, and so on. It can be assembled into macroscopic-scale ensembles that hew to statistical and other laws, and at its most elementary level it devolves into elementary *bits* of information that must obey the laws of quantum information—bits which we'll dub here 'atoms' of information.) At those levels, information cannot be destroyed, but can be deployed and/or re-assembled into ever novel configurations.

Under the laws that govern information, a consciousness made up of information can never be wholly annihilated, *even*, perhaps somewhat surprisingly, in the materialistic scenario. Instead, it may break down into no longer associated, or very loosely or remotely associated, atoms of information—into the information equivalents of Gottfried Leibnitz's consciousness monads—which then become available anew for recycling, and may separately become the constituent elements of new macro-consciousnesses, themselves once again temporary assemblies of myriad available monads. Under this scenario, the billions of atoms of consciousness that used to make up a now deceased person are now released and available to become embedded into new temporary consciousness constructs, such as may make up thousands or millions of now living people or even animals. As it were, your great great grandfather would then, under this scenario, be a little bit present in most everybody you meet.

Under the alternative spiritual scenario, this combination problem does not exist. The more vibrantly alive, more intensely conscious entities are simply bigger spikes off the low consciousness baseline (and as we'll see in Chapter 8, the whole business of the universe seems to consist in lifting the baseline and creating ever more, ever taller spikes.) The 'consciousness spike off the baseline' that is *you* endures, and will henceforth avail itself of every opportunity to do the spiritual universe's bidding—to wit, grow ever further by any conceivable means available, be it some form of renewed existence within some material domain, sometimes but not necessarily indistinguishable from the concept of reincarnation, or migration to other, perhaps subtler realms—whatever floats its boat. The recombination problem exists only if panpsychism is taken to mean that all that exists are 'atoms' of consciousness, all with a same consciousness profile. Yet, that is not what panpsychism means : all it means is the existence of an all-pervading baseline of consciousness. The richer scenario of a potentially infinite number of different consciousness profiles off the all-pervading baseline effectively eliminates the issue. (Some of the philosophers who adopt the spiritual scenario still take the view that a consciousness spike can be temporarily broken or partly deconstructed, thereby blending elements of both. Unconventional therapists such as Itzhtak Beery or dream therapist and author Robert Moss, for example, and others believe that traumatic experiences can fragment a person's consciousness, with bits then leaving that person, and that one goal of therapy is to reunite the errant bits to the main consciousness and make it whole again.)

Incidentally, the difference between full-blown spikes of consciousness capable of evolution and changeless 'atoms of consciousness' may shed light on the oft-debated question of whether AI systems can become conscious, in other words whether artificial systems can develop independent spike-level consciousness.

From a panpsychic perspective, all that may be vanishingly conscious in some simple material things—a stone, a lump of metal, or, say, a chair—are the *particles* that compose them. Although these particles, which under panpsychism are each seen as bearers of rudimentary consciousness, are loosely interlinked by the agency of having to remain within a set distance of one another, they however most likely do not combine elementary consciousnesses to yield up some consciousness at a higher level : a chair remains a collection of disparate particles and does not become aware or intelligent at some higher level of consciousness.

There of course exist other, more conscious systems than loose collections of particles, the world's animals and plants[xi]. As is described in a number of resources, these more evolved systems feature spikes of consciousness off a universal, low consciousness baseline. In their case, consciousness does not arise from a recombination of basic constituent consciousness elements, *aka* 'atoms of consciousness' or sometimes 'monads of consciousness', but it arises, grows and evolves through a fully different mechanism, and there is no recombination issue, because the mechanism giving rise to higher levels of consciousness does not take its source in the combination of elementary consciousness atoms. The ability to grow independently, without the intervention and/or agency of a third party, is the immediately observable key difference between these two kinds of systems. Plants and animals do that. Stones and lumps of metal and silicon crystals do not. Hence, a conclusion might be that AI systems will only develop their own form of spike consciousness the instant they become able to independently grow/repair themselves/shoot out new system parts and/or subroutines, without the agency and/or intervention of anyone. Until then, AI systems will remain no more conscious than a chair or a stone, even though the *appearance* of consciousness can easily be programmed in.

How do individual spikes come to be? In other words, how does any individual consciousness, largely independent and never fully separate from the universal consciousness, get to be born? An intriguing possibility would be a slightly unstable, ever-so-faintly jittering baseline, where random tiny spikes would pop in and out of existence, perhaps both under and above the main profile line—thereby mirroring the omnipresent quantum vacuum itself, where virtual particles, along with more exotic virtual elements such as bubbles of time or space, continuously pop in and out of existence. Because the baseline stands under a faint overall upwards pressure which applies at all times—that's why the universe exists in the first place—some of the small random up-kinks may start separating out and growing, and lo and behold—perhaps some new fruit fly or some rudimentary-consciousness equivalent has thereby been born into existence. As it turns out, solid evidence exists that insects are theoretically capable of individual consciousness, as shown by Australian researchers Colin Klein and Andrew B. Barron–a result also borne out by experiments in which insects deal with situations which their instincts cannot possibly have prepared them for[xii].

There is also experimental evidence that humans are dimly in touch with one another via a shared low consciousness baseline : Roger D. Nelson, a psychologist formerly with Princeton University, ran the 'Global Consciousness Project'[xiii] which showed that the output of hardware-generated true-random numbers is statistically significantly affected by global events, whenever they are momentous enough to capture the attention and the emotions of vast numbers of people across the world : randomly generated number profiles consistently stray from their usual patterns whenever events that carry an emotional charge, such as the death of Princess Diana, gain worldwide exposure. The effect transcends both space (deviations from pure profile randomness appear everywhere on Earth, regardless of where the causing event occurs) and more intriguingly time (the deviations may appear before the causing event.) Biologist Rupert Sheldrake documented a similar phenomenon of remote mindlike networking amongst animals, observing that often, when a member of one species somewhere hits upon some innovative way to do something (such as find a new source of food), the new item of knowledge quickly spreads to the rest of the species, even when there is no direct contact between the animals. In Japan, a group of apes learned to break open a fruit using a stone. At almost the same time, other ape groups in faraway Congo and New Guinea began exhibiting the same behavior. Similar observations have been made with birds and other animals[xiv]. It would therefore be interesting to devise a means of checking whether animal and human consciousnesses are able to achieve a measure of interspecies contact, rather than narrowly humans with humans, and animals with other members of their species. Since humankind-wide reaction to events causing widespread deaths and terror seem to be reliably repeatable, it would certainly be interesting to test whether animal-kingdom wide reactions to such things as the Yulin dogmeat festival or the Faroese dolphin cull would be observed too—but of course what urgently needs to happen instead, is that such things stop once and for all.

*

3–There absolutely exists *non-physical* information.

For Oxford University information theorist Vlatko Vedral and many others, *everything* is information—there is no such thing as independent matter or independent energy, and everything ultimately boils down to information. This view, combined with physicist Paul Davies's and others' view that "all life is information" and reversely that pure information defines life, neatly gibes with the panpsychism we encountered earlier: everything is alive. Although a calculation by Rolf Landauer shows that some modicum of energy is always necessarily attached to the transmission and reception of information (there is some unsettled ongoing debate as to the calculated threshold values of such energy), there exist configurations where information exists but, as it were, is held in abeyance for possible future use and not necessarily transmitted or accessed : the lack of access to or use of information does not destroy it.

More information is proven to exist in the world than the information that can be materially accessed, and/or that is embedded within material substrates : in mathematics, Holevo's bound sets an upper limit on the amount of information that can be retrieved from any store of information held within a quantum system, and the quantum system holds more information that can be retrieved from it : in keeping with Paul Davies's aphorism that life is information, it means that *some life is not material*. Some of it must exist in discarnate quantum realms, in other words in the 'smoky part of the dragon', and no mechanism exists that can force it to ever incarnate. More information—or life—can be contained within the immaterial part of a system than in its physical part. A similar conclusion had been reached via a slightly different route (in quoted ref 6), that of a physics based novel view of consciousness.

A broadly equivalent way exists to illustrate the point : look at the information contained in a dream. A dream undeniably contains information, that of its scenario, much like a Hollywood film script holds information. A dream can however either be remembered by its dreamer (even vaguely), or not at all. In the latter case, information still exists somewhere out there—information cannot be destroyed—but since it can never be accessed or retrieved it isn't material at all—much like Holevo's bound prevents all of the information contained within a quantum system from ever becoming fully accessible from within a material environment. In the case when the dreamer remembers their dream, even sketchily, some energy will indeed be expended by the brain to recall it, as the brain's memory circuits fire up in its process of recollection.

*

4—Last but not least, Ockham's razor is unable to decide in favor of the simpler materialistic scenario.

Ockham's razor, which holds that if some phenomenon can be logically explained by one of several contending explanations, then the simpler explanation must be the correct one, is not always valid, and can on occasion be quite misleading : Lawrence Krauss, in his intriguing book '*A Universe Out of Nothing*', shows how the cosmologists of a distant future would *inevitably* reach all the utterly wrong conclusions about how the universe came to be if they applied Ockham's razor.

Looking back in history, there have been many cases when the more involved explanation of some phenomenon has proven to be true, and the simpler explanation wrong. Lord Kevin, the preeminent physicist of his time, famously said that 'all of physics' was known, and that all that was left to ever do henceforth was to refine some constants to a few more decimal places—just *before* the twin revolutions of quantum physics and relativity took place, that would upend everything Lord Kelvin knew about physics. Mistakes or misapprehensions can also stem from a number of well-known shortcomings : insidious cognitive bias is a frequent culprit, as is the failure to take into account or even glimpse the relevant wider picture. As a case in point, it is Thomas Watson, the then head of IBM, opining that the worldwide market for computers amounted to a grand total of five, if that, or the Nobel prize winning economist Paul Krugman stating that the overall impact of the internet on the economy would be less than that of the fax machine. The common thread in all of those mistakes was that the correct view could only be seen from within a bigger picture that did not exist yet, so unfamiliar that it was unimaginable.

It is thus often the *richer* explanation that tends to be the valid one, and it consistently overrides Ockham's razor : ours is a rich and complex universe. Richness opens up new realms where nature's endless creativity and diversity can blossom out and expand untrammeled. Ockham's razor tends to prove true between two *equally rich* alternatives—but if one of the alternatives opens up a whole new universe of possibilities and potential for exploration, then that alternative is most likely the correct one. This general principle holds true on many levels, including at the ground level of ordinary human experience : complexity and richness trump and enable much. If you are allowed to, say, enjoy or study music, you'll then, and only then, get to know which genre you resonate with if any, or which instrument you may have an unsuspected talent for, because you are in a position to explore realms of achievement that you would not otherwise have suspected the existence and the thrill of. As William Blake had famously put it, the roads of excess lead to the palaces of wisdom. Opening doors to experience leads to complex, unforeseen worlds of exploration and knowledge, to talents taking wing. It may even cross-fertilize and foster better understanding in other, unrelated areas. In physics, the starkly counterintuitive and un-simple explanations which quantum mechanics provided of certain small phenomena at the edges of measurements proved true, against the far more pedestrian explanations which applying Ockham's razor would have suggested.

There used to be an unexpected guideline at the cutting edge of physics, the place where different theories compete to separately make sense of some observed phenomenon, but where a smoking gun to settle matters once and for all remains elusive, be it theoretically or experimentally : *beauty*. In his 2002 anthology titled *'It Must Be Beautiful'*, Graham Farmelo collated twelve well-known physicists' pieces, setting forth how a sense of beauty, of resonance with a harmoniously built universe, serves as a valid guideline in the search for scientific truth. (Since then, the idea has come in for a rather merciless pounding by the likes of Sabine Hossenfelder and others, and is no longer quite as prevalent as it used to be.) Above and beyond the descriptive equations of an observed reality, where beauty can still play a role as a soft guide (no one has ever encountered an ugly, yet correct equation), I would submit that in terms of looking for *places where to look*—as opposed to looking within already well-trodden areas of science and fields of enquiry—*richness* must constitute a strong guide. George Bernard Shaw was more right than he knew when he said "There are those that look at things the way they are, and ask why. I dream of things that never were, and ask, why not?"- a thought that beautifully applies to science discovery. The history of mathematics itself is replete with such instances, as leaps of imagination into richer realms time and again opened the floodgates to uncommon progress, beginning with the invention of naught—a cipher invented several times independently under different climes and, as far as we can tell, much derided on every single occasion. Nearer to us in time, the invention of the rather ill-named imaginary numbers (the square roots of negative numbers), explored and developed against much shrill opposition from the then mathematical establishment. These numbers absolutely exist, of course, they just happen to be literally in a different place than more ordinary numbers. Whole branches of engineering (electrical, electronic) would not have been developed if it hadn't been for those numbers. (Thankfully, they tend to be nowadays called 'complex numbers' rather than 'imaginary'. In turn, they have given rise to new kinds of numbers, the quaternions and other hypercomplex number systems, which in turn are opening up new branches of enquiry and mathematics.)

Rich is the new beautiful, and when Ockham's razor fails, new paradigms are often born.

In summary, this is where we have now arrived :

1. Matter is an illusion : everything ultimately entirely boils down to pure, immaterial mathematics.
2. Not all of information is material. Vast hoards of extant information are neither accessible from, nor containable within, a material environment
3. Consciousness is not emergent but the fundamental feature of reality, even seated atop mathematics in the hierarchy of reality (as per the Auguste Lecomte ranking.)
4. Reality most often proves richer than we may think from the standpoint of our cognitive biases.

3 Other Views

There have been, and there are many other earnest efforts to understand the world and what makes it tick, and there exists a resultant vast body of literature reflecting such efforts. This literature, a record of thoughts reaching back in time all the way up to the present, seeks to address, from a wide variety of angles, how we ought to understand the world and the universe, and although much of it is not in keeping with either one of the two above scenarios, they still certainly rate mentioning.

In quite general terms, to appreciate how majority views on any subject can emerge from within groups of people collaboratively seeking to understand some phenomenon and/or devise useful ways of dealing with some reality, it helps to first take a detour via a TV reality show called '*Traitors*'. The show exemplifies how often and how fast attempts at collectively understanding anything are apt to go astray, and therefrom how poor the solutions devised to deal with some issue can turn out to be—an issue that has been, as History amply demonstrates, the scourge of human society since time immemorial. It continues to plague the way we attempt to deal with things; It is the very issue that has led to the advent of so many "-isms", a great deal of which ended up visiting pain and devastation on humankind rather than providing solutions.

In 'Traitors', a group of players, more or less randomly selected from entrants from the public, compete for a sum of money over the course of a few days (a kitty to which they add every day by successfully carrying out some set tasks, and which by the end of the game typically amounts to well over a hundred thousand dollars, making it well worth reaching for.) Most of the players are so-called 'faithfuls', and two or three are secretly 'traitors'. It is in the interest of the 'faithfuls'—the majority of the players—that the 'traitors' in their midst be uncovered and eliminated, because if any traitor remains at the end of the game, she or he will keep the whole amount in the money kitty and any remaining faithfuls shall be left with nothing, whereas if no traitor is left, the remaining faithfuls will share the kitty equally amongst themselves. Every day, someone is eliminated from the game, either voted out on suspicion of being a traitor by a simple majority of the players' votes during a daily elimination round, or removed from the game overnight, by secret diktat of the traitors who have the right to eliminate one player every day. The purpose of the faithfuls is to urgently identify who the traitors are, and to eliminate them from the game by voting them out.

So far, so good.

Where it becomes fascinating is how the players weave incredibly elaborate, incredibly cogent and logical theories about who might be—who must be—a traitor, so that they can vote them out in the daily 'banishment vote'.

And they get it entirely, woefully wrong every time.

Which neatly encapsulates much of the history of human civilization : cogent and logical philosophies and/or "-isms", thought up at much expense of collaborative brainpower and thought leadership, most often designed to tackle society's issues, needs and challenges, but also on occasion merely to unveil nature's secrets, which have led to all manner of religions, social philosophies and/or -isms, such as—to give but a couple of examples from a vast pool of failed ideas once held to be panacea—cults or religions that prescribed human sacrifices or mutilation, or more recently fascism and communism and many other such, all of which may have sounded solidly logical and appeared impeccable on paper, yet turned out to be woefully, terribly, pathetically wrong. At least in the TV reality game all is soon revealed and the theories tested against reality itself, as it is soon revealed whether an eliminated player is indeed a traitor or not. No such luck in the real world, where -isms are tried out and typically wreak havoc before they are at long last recognized for what they are : wrong, fanciful and far removed from reality. As Barack Obama once put it, 'Reality has a way of asserting itself', and sometimes it does so at a terrible price.

'Traitors' illustrates a sobering truth about human understanding : we may attempt to think as hard as we possibly can, as logically as we are able, on the basis of all of the data we can work out and identify and collate, and yet there is still zero guarantee that we'll be right. A significant part of the reason why has to be that we can never have access to all of the relevant data, or even easily or reliably understand or know what the relevant data is. As Donald Rumsfeld had famously put it, "There are things we know that we know. There are known unknowns. That is to say, things that we know we don't know. But there are also unknown unknowns : things we don't know we don't know."

There is even a mathematical reason why, even if we had all of the data pertaining to a specific issue or situation, we would not even necessarily devise the best or the right or the optimal way to deal with it : there are always more possible, mathematically sound ways of dealing with any amount of data – even an infinite amount. A little-known bane of progress in science is that many different and contradictory mathematical solutions can seamlessly fit any possible collection of experimental data points : all we ever have from observation is a collection of data points – but there is a strong infinity of mathematical functions that can seamlessly fit any possible collection of data points, no matter whether finite or infinite, and the infinity of suitable mathematical functions capable of fitting any collection of data points, is a stronger infinity (i.e., infinitely bigger, technically at the aleph-2 mark) than even any infinity of data points (forever stuck at the aleph-0 mark.) Here is a simple way of illustrating this with a mere 9 data points : what is the next point in the series y= 1,2,3,4,5,6,7,8 ? Say that these points are plotted on an (x,y) graph at (x=1,y=1), (x=2,y=2) etc., and the next point on the plot at y= 9 is hidden by an overlaid piece of cardboard. Although you'd be tempted to say, on the basis of the known sequence of the first 8 points, that the next point is logically at y= 9, it absolutely need not be the case, and the belief that the next point is logically at y=9 is little else than cognitive bias, born of a human tendency to see and discern patterns where there are none. Indeed, there exist an *infinity* of valid plots that go through all these early 8 points and then any possible next value after y= 8 : even though the apparently *simplest* value of y at x=9 could be deemed to be 9, the very concept of 'simplest' is judgment-dependent and cognitively biased, and there is no reason why it should be the actual real-world value. There is just no way to know the actual value Y of the next point at (x=9,y=Y) without confrontation with reality—that is, by lifting the cardboard overlay and taking a peek. The number of possible real-world solutions to any given real-world problem can *only* be brought down from the infinity of possible, legitimate math-only solutions by experimentation—i.e., by testing against reality.

Most of the traditional literature that seeks to understand how the world, human life, and/or the universe work, does so from a variety of angles, broadly classifiable into one of three categories :

1. Religious views, often colored by a confessional or denominational angle
2. Traditional materialistic views, *and*
3. Everything else, including spiritual but nonreligious approaches, and more recently other views such as the simulation hypothesis, according to which the whole universe including ourselves are just parts of an advanced, hyper-realistic computer simulation, possibly run and overseen by some ill-defined higher being or beings.

Irrespective of any particular angle, some issues seem to arise time and again.

A first issue is that, as an old saw puts it, to the man with a hammer, everything looks like a nail. To a deeply religious Marist monk, everything appears to be somehow correlated to the purported role and interventions in the world of the Virgin Mary. To a video game developer, everything will be reminiscent of properties and features associated with video games. To a software developer, everything will resonate with software development, tools, and capabilities. To an information scientist, everything will be seen in relation to how information may play out, including at the weird fringes of what information science may allow.

And in every single case, just like the Traitors players, they will all find plenty to prop up their views. And in many, many cases, said views will be either plain wrong or at the very least incomplete. And the bigger picture—the much wider realities outside their preferred purviews and areas of competence—shall remain ignored.

The 'miracle' of the levitating host captured on video during the November 7th, 1999 Catholic Mass service at the minor Basilica of Lourdes, France, neatly illustrates how interpretations from an angle can work. The Mass ceremony was celebrated by Cardinals Louis-Marie Billé and Jean-Marie Lustiger, attended by a number of French bishops, a number of priests and the superiors of Trappist monasteries worldwide, and broadcast live on French television. On the altar lay two hosts (thin ceremonial wafers) meant to be consecrated. At the beginning of the Mass, the two hosts appear in the film stacked one above the other, so that one cannot clearly tell that there are two instead of one. They are resting on the paten, a type of tray, and are neatly stacked up. The film shows various camera angles showing them in this position and there is no doubt that the two hosts are physically stacked one atop the other and resting on the paten. At the moment of the so-called "epiclesis", when the priest extends his hands and invokes the Holy Spirit, the upper host detaches from the lower one and levitates. It assumes a stable horizontal position, suspended about half an inch high, and stays in this position until the end of the Canon.

These are the hard facts. They can be easily interpreted to fit any desired narrative, in mutually wholly incompatible ways, as follows :

- The Catholic monk may interpret the event as a clear intervention by either God or a Catholic saint or some other holy figure (such as an angel.) He will easily point to many other cases confirming this view.
- The stimulation hypothesis proponent interprets this as a glitch in the matrix—a slippage in the fabric of apparent reality, caused by a temporary software error, confirming the suspicion that no software program can ever be entirely flawless, not even that of the hugely advanced beings that run the simulation behind the scenes. They will easily point to many other cases supporting this thesis.
- 19th century-style, as well as more recent materialists will scoff at the naivety of gullible people so easily taken in by fraud, or by errant air drafts, or whatever the cause may be, and will point at the utter meaninglessness of a floating piece of thin, ultra-light wafer, and wonder how anyone could believe that some deity would bother with such ridiculously childish pranks. They will easily point to many other cases buttressing this interpretation.
- Some information theoreticians will say that the laws of physics do not pre-exist but spring up at the same time as the phenomenon they measure, and that therefore it is entirely inevitable that some phenomena will fail to conform to how physical laws happen to pop up most of the time. They will easily find other cases bearing out this viewpoint.

A true or complete view of reality can hardly be reached from a narrow, parochial standpoint. From experience gained from trawling through vast swathes of the relevant literature, I'd venture to say that one major, recurrent flaw plagues many attempted, but failed or incomplete explanations of reality : they ignore the fundamental hidden feature of material reality, which is that matter is not fundamental. In keeping with John Wheeler's image of a smoky dragon, matter is made up of a small amount of tangible material (technically, collapsed wave-functions), and of a much bigger, immaterial component (uncollapsed wave functions)—many garden-variety analyses and attempts at explaining the world overlook the 'smoky middle part of the dragon', which nevertheless not only constitutes the vast majority of the dragon's body—meaning the vast majority of reality, but also the part which material reality can toggle back to, and which more importantly governs, behind the material scenes, how the hard extremities of the dragon will conduct themselves—in other words, how material reality behaves when it is in its material state.

Another significant issue is that of so-called *spurious correlations* : some things happen to seem closely correlated or associated but are in fact not at all—and conclusions are apt to be drawn that are in no way warranted. The resource at[xv] gives stunning examples such as the very close correlations *over decades* of such things as, variously, the use of GMO corn in Michigan with the number of registrations of Yamaha motorbikes in the UK, the number of bachelor's degrees in library science with the number of Google searches for 'How to hide a body', the number of UFO sightings in South Carolina with the total number of successful Mount Everest climbs—among many other equally astonishing instances. Anyone with an agenda—or as the case may be, perhaps overly naive—can use such data to build a serious-sounding, yet wholly nonsensical case about anything. It seems to me that it is a sin the simulation hypothesis is guilty of, and I have to agree here with those, such as Sabine Hossenfelder and others, who deem it a pseudo-science.

4 Consciousness

Fate and destiny and can only ever attach to a sentience, a *consciousness*. Many physicists, including luminaries such as Max Planck, Erwin Schrödinger, Heinrich Päs, et al. have concluded that not only consciousness is the only reality but also that there can exist only *one* consciousness, for which some arguments suggest that it is most likely infinite in some of its features, a question we will turn to in Chapter 6. Other physicists, such as Eugene Wigner, John von Neumann, and others, while not explicitly stating the existence of only one consciousness, espouse views that can best be explained by the existence of a unified consciousness throughout the universe. From a quite different angle, philosophers including well-known contemporary ones such as above-cited Philip Goff, building their case from the vantage point of modern arguments, have presented solid arguments reaching the same conclusion[xvi]. Finally, for those who lean towards accepting the presence of a more traditional monotheist God rather than the lesser god arising over time from the 'materialistic' scenario above, there exists a confirming mathematical argument that says that such God would necessarily be omnipresent and pervade the whole of creation, rather than only dwell at certain privileged locations in multidimensional spacetime, thereby finally settling the old debate between immanence and transcendence that has been the object of debate by theologians since time immemorial[xvii].

The purpose of human life is usually seen as falling into either one of three broad, mutually exclusive alternatives.

1. There is no purpose, humans and for that matter all life forms are temporary assemblies of atoms and molecules that will soon fade back into the nothingness whence they sprang. Meanwhile, day-to-day lives are mostly determined by random events, or by the unforeseeable consequences of small insignificant events—as famously

depicted in the *Sliding Doors* movie, where the life of the main protagonist played by Gwyneth Paltrow unfolds in totally different directions depending upon whether she catches a subway coach, or has to wait for the next one because of a few seconds' tardiness. Unbeknownst to them, the interplay of random events across the world intertwines many lives, and that's all there is.

2. Humans are the apex henchmen of the cosmos, the short-lived by-products of a universe created by the laws of mathematics, devised to help efficiently redress, and keep redressing, the mathematical imbalances that arise as a result of its creation. In their ceaseless efforts to make their own lives better, healthier, and longer, they unwittingly do the cosmos's mechanical bidding and accelerate its conversion of free energy into mild undifferentiated heat.
3. Humans are the co-citizens of a live, conscious cosmos. Everlasting consciousness pervades everything, it is all that remains after the non-essential layers of reality are stripped away. The existence of matter, time, and of the whole apparent shebang of material reality is just the way this wide-ranging consciousness intermediates itself into situations where, for lack of a better word, experience is gained. Our lives are meaningful and unspool in a way that contributes to the whole cosmos growing in wisdom. In Carl Sagan 's words, '*We are a way for the universe to know itself*'. Most of seeming randomness may not be truly random, a point made in innumerable popular novels as well as in many works of nonfiction[xviii].

But why should 'experience be gained'?

As it happens, mathematics hints both at a reason why, and at how :

- There are solid arguments suggesting that our known finite universe is part of a wider, infinite universe. Going into these reasons is beyond the scope of this book, but other resources make the point[xix].

- This universe is a fully-mathematical universe, despite appearing to be material. Drill down into matter, from a pure physics point of view, and all you're left with are discarnate mathematical objects, such as functions and numbers, which hew to the ever abiding laws of mathematics—and nothing else.
- This raises the question of whether mathematics is the ultimate reality, sufficient unto itself, or whether it is part of, or underpropped by, something else. As we saw in Chapter 2, mindstuff takes precedence over mathematics.
- Although it may be counterintuitive, it is a mathematical fact that there exists an infinity of different infinities, and that all infinities, irrespective of their attributes, are always capable of further growth. There is no such thing as an infinity (technically, at any aleph metric) that cannot grow further.
- If some infinity—such as the probable infinity of, or of some of its attributes, of the universal consciousness—does not grow, it becomes static, for all intents and purposes *dead*—just like, say, any collection of objects, no matter how huge, to which new items would never be added would become static, frozen in time—in effect henceforth 'dead' and museum-like.
- In order to grow, everything including infinity needs something impelling them to grow : a growth engine. Physics shows that any possible engine of growth can only be something that takes advantage of a lack of equilibrium somewhere–or, in technical terms, that obeys the second law of thermodynamics. If perfect balance is achieved within a medium or environment, it cannot fuel movement and can neither stimulate nor beget growth. An arena where the second law of thermodynamics can superbly work its wonders is an imperfect, material universe : just like ours.
- Therefore, there must exist some environment similar to ours (a world or a universe) so that infinity, or at least some

> of its constituents, can continue to grow, and thereby that it never becomes static and museum-like.

Experience is gained in order to prevent consciousness from becoming museum-like. In starker yet equivalent words, to *prevent consciousness from dying*.

Whether embedded within some material being or not, consciousness features various degrees of intensity, answering to the representative height of the consciousness spike off the universal consciousness baseline which any particular sentient being is made of. In turn, its quality-meaning how consciousness would deploy itself into the material world—would critically depend on the attributes of the particular material it embeds itself in—how such material matrix may allow for the deploying, harnessing and use of the immense range of capabilities that pure consciousness seems otherwise able to proffer. As it happens, a key role of the brain is the *curbing* of the capabilities of pure consciousness. Whenever this curbing or filtering function is impaired, otherwise dormant extraordinary abilities are apt to emerge. If the rest of the brain remains unaffected and only its filtering function is damaged, then people may variously recall in full detail every single instant of their lives, as Jill Price has in excruciating detail since 1974, others affected with other forms of brain dysfunction will go into their particular 'zone' and, say, correctly reel off the number pi (π) to tens of thousands of decimal digits, as world champion Akira Haraguchi has done to an incredible over 110,000 correct consecutive digits, or Vemuri Sai Akshara who recites the square root of 2 to thousands of decimal places when blindfolded. Many so-called savants, such as Daniel Tammet and many others, achieve similar feats. When in addition to its filtering functions, other parts of the brain are also damaged or in any way impaired, people can become challenged by simple, everyday tasks such as tying their shoes, yet nevertheless still exhibit extraordinary abilities, as was famously portrayed in the 1988 Hollywood film 'Rain Man' featuring Dustin Hoffman and Tom Cruise. What a consciousness even partly loosened from its usual moorings can achieve is nothing short of spectacular : any normal person, even one with an above Mensa-level IQ, could not dream of emulating even a vanishingly small part of such performances.

Humans all have different personality make-ups and are apt to think markedly differently. For that matter, any given individual's personality and modes of thought constantly evolve over time : anyone's consciousness spike evolves constantly, all part of a universal consciousness trying out so many different paths to growth. Contributory destinies play themselves out within the material universe.

5 Building Knowledge

From the standpoint of the universe that produced us, our individual purpose in life is to keep growing in both knowledge and wisdom, thereby either contributing to raising universal consciousness, under the richer, more spiritual scenario depicted in Chapter 2, or simply as a means of acquiring tools enabling us to keep surviving, and hence serve the purpose of efficiently converting energy for longer, as per the materialistic scenario of Chapter 1. Reasonable people routinely reach quite different conclusions from looking at the exact same phenomena and data, which tells us that before we can objectively look at a few odd phenomena in the next chapter, and their possible explanations and roles in their wider contexts, we must briefly look at how the knowledge that governs our understanding and the wisdom that informs our worldviews are acquired.

Wisdom requires, and grows with rising levels of both knowledge and maturity : knowledge without maturity does not equate to wisdom (or, as the medieval writer Rabelais had famously put it, *Knowledge without conscience is but the ruination of the soul*), and neither can maturity be attained in ignorance. Wisdom is endlessly extensible : there is no end to its knowledge component in a growing, infinite, multidimensional universe. As for maturity—it probably correlates with experience rather than to general knowledge per se, much like, say, in the business world, a young whippersnapper armed with a fresh top-school MBA will, at the beginning of his or her career, likely not be nearly as savvy and effective as a much less educated but older hand at business. Overall, wisdom cannot be neatly pinned down or measured into neat boxes : one could certainly perceive two elders of vastly different backgrounds, life experiences and bodies of knowledge acquired over lifetimes as being similarly wise, so that any 'wisdom index' yardstick would have to be multi-variables in a way hardly amenable to simple formulas. Through growing wisdom far and wide, the universe gets to know itself.

Before it eventually becomes consensual and verified, knowledge typically winds through a tortuous road where many different takes on reality contend. During that interim period when truth has not yet set into commonly accepted knowledge, all kinds of opinions exist—including fiercely held opinions contradictory to other opinions held every bit as fiercely by equally qualified and equally reasonable individuals. The 'poster men' for different opinions here could be, say, Neil deGrasse Tyson in one corner, averring that 'consciousness does not exist', and a host of theoretical physicists in the other corner, averring that consciousness is all there is and that ultimately, nothing else exists. We could of course pick any one of many other themes, say free will instead of consciousness, or for that matter any number of other fundamental or existential questions for which stalwart proponents are many on both sides. What gives?

Current *aggregate* human knowledge is impressively extensive. To get a feel for it, visit any midsize or larger brick-and-mortar bookshop (luckily, there are still a few around.) What you'll see is hundreds upon hundreds of new books, most of which you likely never knew of, nor had you ever heard of their authors. Arbitrarily choose ten books to read, no matter whether fiction or nonfiction (as the saying goes, fiction is the way to tell the truth through falsehoods, and nonfiction the way to tell falsehoods from truths, so that both genres contain real knowledge and wisdom.) At least half of the books you picked at random will turn out to be excellent : you were missing out on them, as we are all missing out on the knowledge and experience embedded in so many other books and other knowledge vehicles. Return to the brick-and-mortar bookshop a mere one week later : most of the books on display the week before have now been freshly replaced by stacks of new ones... Open public visibility of knowledge and its wide dissemination tend to occur only within narrow time windows and limited shelf lives. Although on-line depositories of knowledge have immensely helped, including online book stores where instead of the few hundreds of books on display at the bricks and mortar, one can now navigate across countless thousands, the visibility algorithms favor the latest and most popular, and as ever a measure of effort is required to access anything off the well-trodden paths.

In Academe, designed to operate as society's main generator of knowledge, the same holds true, with added intensity : no one can possibly, in the 21st century, know everything within any given narrow field of specialization, nor keep abreast of every valuable development within a chosen field. Mathematician Keith Devlin observes that in his field of mathematics, the number of different and contributory textbooks now stands at well beyond one hundred thousand. The number of academic, well-researched, value-adding papers published every *day* on any narrow topic in physics or mathematics or psychology or medicine runs into the thousands. Every year, over 2 million new research articles are published in more than 30,000 peer-reviewed journals across all fields of study. In medicine alone, over 10,000 scientific and research publications are published worldwide every *day*, and no specialist can keep up with all the developments at the forefront of their specialty. Putting things in perspective, biochemist and winner of the Nobel prize in medicine Katalin Kariko, an extremely avid reader of science papers, says she's read about 10,000 papers in her life to-date (and that most of these papers were worthwhile and contributory), answering to the number of papers published every single *day* in her field of medicine.

Unavoidably, not *all* papers are worthwhile, and since the knowledge generation system is such that publications are key to career advancement, sometimes unworthy papers slip through the peer-review process, leading peer-reviewed journals to retract thousands of papers every year. Moreover, journal publishing is also a business, which has led Professor Marcus Munafo of Bristol University and others to warn that the twinning of the imperative to 'publish or perish' for researchers on the one hand, with the journals' ongoing need for a steady stream of new papers providing revenue on the other hand, creates a perfect storm enabling a measure of bogus research to slip through—and pollute the knowledge generation machinery. Perhaps worse than the bogus research, and in any event sadder, is the occasional well-meant research that happens to be demonstrably wrong, and which before it is picked up as such wreaks havoc on the understanding and ultimately worldview of countless readers. Yet, despite whatever warts and blemishes there may be, the system broadly works. Medicine, for instance, or dentistry, have objectively become enviably advanced : in most places, by the time anyone reaches their mid to late adulthood, most of their kith and kin are still alive and well, complete with a full set of beautiful pearly whites—a very recent and welcome set of affairs in the 300,000-odd year history of the human race.

At the softer edges of human enquiry, where the more philosophical questions of purpose, destiny, and eschatology dwell, knowledge generation is slower—no doubt because such knowledge is far less utilitarian than readily actionable knowledge in, say, engineering or medicine. Philosophical science cannot either easily circumvent the issues that will inevitably beset a discipline not directly amenable to experimental confirmation, and the inescapable teething problems associated with the development of any science, as described in Thomas Kuhn's *The Structure of Scientific Revolutions*, are therefore amplified. Moreover, the lack of easily verifiable, and thence readily consensual answers to philosophical questions is apt to open the door to *bias*—pre-existing inner convictions rather than facts informing or even stealthily predetermining views. Whether subconsciously or not, confirmation bias may then set in and data substantiating one's views become primarily or selectively taken into account.

The sheer impossibility to keep abreast of all developments in any field or area of enquiry leads to what has to be the biggest issue in knowledge management and utilization : plain ignorance or lack of awareness, of a relevant bit of knowledge, including as may stem from unrelated fields, as cross-fertilization often proves essential to progress. A first clue is given by the observation that psychologists seem to be as a rule more reductionist than physicists. Do physicists know something that psychologists do not? Since physics is more fundamental than psychology, the answer could well be yes. Thankfully, cross-fertilization happens more and more today than used to be the case even in the recent past, and human knowledge and understanding are expanding at an ever faster clip. As a case in point, Peter Millican, a philosopher at Oxford University, or Nick Yeung, a neuroscientist at the Department of Experimental Psychology at the same University, and others emphasize the crucial role of mathematics in their respective disciplines, and how intensely it is both taught in their departments and used in their fields—which at first sight would seem to not stand in need of much mathematics.

In another but telling case in point, philosopher Philip Goff makes the rather extraordinary claim in his recent book '*Why*' that some form of rudimentary consciousness must play a role in how electrons behave, at least under certain circumstances. Which is, surprisingly enough, exactly what the hard physics—the pure mathematics—says.

How it works can be illustrated by a simple question—how and why does a football (or for that matter a bullet or an arrow or an electron or any projectile that is not self-propelled), an object that has exactly zero memory nor any consciousness of how it was kicked and when and with which impetus, still 'know' over time in which direction and with which force or speed to go as a consequence of that kick? The question may not be entirely straightforward to grasp—most people when asked the question would probably shrug and answer something along the lines of 'well it's obvious, it's where the ball was kicked'—but if we think about it for a minute, we must realize that this pat answer does not work at all.

To appreciate why not, let's do the following thought experiment. Some kind of futuristic operation has left John with vastly enhanced eyesight and extraordinarily capable neural signal-processing abilities to match. John is now able to clearly see a snapshot of anything before his eyes when he bats his eyelids from a shut-eye position back to a shut-eye position within less than a billionth of a second. In an experiment, someone fires a perfectly spherical bullet in front of John's face when his eyes are shut, and he bats his eyelids : what he catches a glimpse of is a perfect metal sphere hanging motionless before his eyes. He has no means whatsoever of knowing where that bullet is going. He has absolutely no clue where the bullet is headed, or at what speed. Yet, needless to say, John has infinitely more memory and more intelligence than the bullet.

How does the bullet know where to go?

The actual answer is astonishing. The object "recalculates" (for lack of a better word) where it should go (i.e., its trajectory) *at every instant in time*. How it quite does that, and exactly what 'every instant in time' may mean (what it is that triggers the instant of the recalculation) is mathematically well understood—although, as is often the case, a more 'physical' explanation is elusive. (As it often turns out, the search for a more 'physical' explanation is often misguided : the mathematics suffices unto itself. If it weren't so, the phenomenon of entanglement, the equivalence of energy and matter embedded in Einstein's equation $e=mc^2$, and a host of other fundamental physics would be incomprehensible. The *mathematics* of entanglement, whereby entangled particles respond to one another *instantly* across astronomical distances, as well as that of $e=mc^2$, is straightforward. Trying to wrap our heads around why such things work in reality is quite another matter. As Eugene Wigner commented once, the power of mathematics in explaining the world appears unreasonable.)

The football, or the bullet, recalculates its trajectory, by means of its associated wave function, which "calculates" everything that pertains to the object (the actual calculations would be far too complex to perform by means of our mathematical symbolism) : in particular, it calculates the *probability of presence* of the football or bullet at any given place in the universe at a given time, and much more besides. The wave function governs at every instant how the object obediently speeds off to its intended destination at the imparted direction and speed and energy with no knowledge of such destination or energy. Actually, not quite : the object dashes off *more or less* to its destination at *more or less* the energy intended – within the error margins of the constant 'recalculating'. As it evolves through time, the wave function recalculates at every 'instant' the object's probability of presence anywhere, along with its other parameters : technically, all of the relevant parameters (position, energy, speed...) take on the instantaneous, evolving, spot values governed by the *boundary conditions* attached to integral terms in the calculation. These boundary conditions evolve over time – they are newly reset at every instant of time, and their values are ever-anew set by what is happening in the object's environment or conditions : a kick causes a change in the values of these boundaries. *The mathematical effect of the kick was to alter the integration's boundary values* and thence the calculation of what the object should do and where it should find itself. The kick did not affect the ball directly, but *indirectly,* via its associated mathematical reality.

Importantly for experimental verification, the self-calculated peak of probability of presence of the object on its desired, or imparted, trajectory is not exactly 100%, and the same applies to all other parameters, such as speed or energy. Experiments have been conducted observing the trajectories of free electrons after they have been emitted by an electron tube. Electrons are so light that fleeting instantaneous random deviations from trajectory can properly be observed, and, because the wave functions of free electrons can be explicitly calculated, their deviations can be computed and statistically predicted. Random instantaneous deviations (which can thus be theoretically predicted) have been observed in experiments and they *behave exactly as is expected from the calculations*—the electrons are observed to continuously stray from their intended path, seeking out their trajectory in real time, and always reverting, more or less, to their intended (imparted) trajectory. The statistics of the experimentally observed deviations from the imparted trajectories, in terms of the directions and amplitudes of deviations, match within a very narrow margin the values expected from the calculations of the wave functions.

The mathematics describes a behavior indistinguishable from how rudimentary consciousness would work.

Relatedly, under the 'free will theorem', first formulated by John Conway and Simon Kochen, the existence of free will in sentient beings implies that elementary particles *must* also have a measure of free will to enable the existence of free will at larger scales, and vice versa : free will is the exact same, indistinguishable phenomenon at all scales and at all levels of material reality (with 'free will' defined as meaning that any decision made at any time is *not* fully determined by anything that has happened or gone on prior to the instant the decision is made). Above and beyond any other considerations, such as earlier-cited arguments by neuroscientist Bobby Azarian and others, this constitutes physical proof that free will is actually for real.

A question of course is, what is it that prompts the wave function's self-recalculation to launch, stop, and begin again? Is there a mechanism that allows this to happen, to in effect isolate and privilege a given succession of otherwise indistinguishable time-points when a wave function executes a continuing series of recalculations? If time is discontinuous within a discrete spacetime, it is relatively easy to conceptualize that a recalculation is reset at each actual instant of present time. Should time however be continuous, then there would hardly exist any starting point capable of providing the trigger for any recalculation—and we are thereby unexpectedly rediscovering Zeno of Citium's logic, who said that if time were infinitely divisible, then motion would be impossible. In any space-time, where the recalculation mechanism would, for whatever reason, *not* be capable of operating, reality would become weird and objects (if such could exist in such a space-time to begin with) would not be able to self-calculate their own wave functions – they would drift about aimlessly, regardless of any past history. A kicked ball or a fired bullet would not know what to do – presumably just float about rudderlessly. Not to worry : our spacetime is discrete, and separate 'instants of time' exist. Carlo Rovelli calculates that there are (1 followed by a hundred zeroes) 'atoms of space' in a centimeter cube of space, and corresponding atoms of time. The old phrase 'spacetime continuum' was only ever an approximation, mostly valid because its granularity is so fine.

6 Intervention

If we adopt the more compelling view laid out in Chapter 2 that we are more than mere deluxe gradient-lowering constructs popping up out of nowhere and soon dissolving back into nothingness, we must wonder why most individual—and collective—destinies prove so tragic. How does that make any sense at all in a universe that seems to be imbued with meaning? If all sentient beings are indeed spikes of consciousness of different profiles off a faint universal baseline of consciousness, and the universe is more than a mere temporary and meaningless phenomenon, then why are the destinies of most sentient beings on Earth so relentlessly tragic? Consciousness does not necessarily equate to any form of intelligence, and it could be that even if broadly faintly aware, the universe is not in any meaningful sense intelligent and hence, at least in its results, does not significantly differ from the materialistic universe. In that picture, universal consciousness would be exclusively made up of an all-pervading low baseline, and the individuals of any species made of spikes of different heights and intensities off that baseline. As we saw earlier, rudimentary small spikes could form spontaneously, giving rise to dimly conscious life forms (such as, in the above example, fruit flies.) Intelligent beings would then constitute sparse instances of more refined consciousness—the life forms responsible over time for most of the heavy lifting of the general raising of consciousness, which under the more spiritual remains scenario the reason for the existence of the universe, no matter whether higher consciousness is an exception or a rule.

A key question is therefore whether the observations we are able to make from our limited standpoint rather point to a largely mindless universe, slowly awakening in consciousness, or instead to a universe whose underlying mindstuff may be extremely advanced, infinite in many of its attributes and metrics, yet still and forever growing. The answer will inform the possible trajectories that our destinies can take. Let's briefly look at the core arguments supporting either alternative, along with how any opposite arguments are interpreted by the other side :

1. Arguments in favor of the first alternative : the universal consciousness (UC), *aka* the universe's underlying mind-stuff, is rudimentary.
    a. All that is needed for a universe of any kind to precipitate into physical reality is the everlasting validity of the laws of mathematics everywhere, including within full nothingness—in the true vacuum, i.e. a vacuum without any residual energy and no quantum effects of any kind. This abiding validity would cause any instance of true vacuum to immediately tunnel into some *false* vacuum (i.e. a quantum vacuum at some nonzero energy state) from its prior state of absolute nothingness, whence a material universe will then eventually arise, most likely via a Big Bang type event. A Big Bang can arise from a variety of quite different scenarios which, billions of years later, would nevertheless lead to the same appearance of a past Big Bang. Physicists Edward Tryon, Roger Penrose, Martin Bojowald, Richard Tolman, Ernst Pascual Jordan, Alex Vilenkin, Peter Bergman, Petro Fomin and a few others have formulated the physics that permit various scenarios which can unleash, at some point, a Big Bang. All of those scenarios are made possible by the existence of something prior to the Big Bang event (even though 'prior to' may take on a different meaning than is commonly understood in a three-dimensional material universe.) The irreducible prior '*something*' that enables these scenarios is the abiding validity of mathematics within a non-material environment.
    b. Although some form of consciousness must underlie mathematics, even a dim consciousness is presumably sufficient to empower at least some of the laws of mathematics. That dim consciousness continues and

pervades the universe after the Big Bang event and constitutes its baseline of consciousness. It's also the reason why life is enabled and sustained by the exact same chemicals that constitute all of supposedly inert matter : there is no difference between live and inert, and panpsychism must rule. The quality of the UC slowly rises over eons of time, in keeping with Carl Sagan's aphorism that *'We are a way for the universe to know itself'*.

c. Despite what thousands of religions have been telling us since the dawn of humankind, the underlying UC is not in any way almighty or all-powerful. This is why so much injustice, so much unjustifiable wanton horror affects and brutalizes millions of souls—*aka* spikes of consciousness. Even some theologians, such as Harold Kushner, have adopted this view[xx].

d. The baseline level of consciousness, together with the many spikes off it embodied in various living beings, keeps rising. Enriched by experience, it is slowly smartening and, against a number of criteria, it becomes sharper and overall, against a set of objective criteria, more intelligent and more aware. At the end of the life of the material universe, some one hundred billion-odd years from now, the universal consciousness embodied within the consciousness baseline in our universe will still continue on, after all things material have dissolved back into near nothingness, inhabiting a new all-pervading false vacuum at a slightly higher residual energy state than was the case before, now at a better level of cognition than was the case before the Big Bang event that gave rise to our universe.

e. A new Big Bang event from the new false vacuum will take place again at some point, and a new universe be born. The still-extant, all-pervading UC will not start from zero in this new universe, but from the level it had reached when the prior universe ended, thereby continuing its upward growth from where it had left off. The new Big Bang could in principle spring from any of the workable scenarios envisioned by various physicists. In the light of the apparent low level of the consciousness baseline in our current universe, it seems to be a young, relatively callow universe, either the first or one of the first universes which, in the fullness of time, will arise that way, steadily contributing to the progressive smartening and betterment of universal consciousness.

f. Because infinity or infinite attributes can never be reached in finite time from finite elements or from a finite seed, UC will never achieve infiniteness, at least not in our universe. It will however keep steadily, endlessly growing.
g. There may exist, or not, other separate universes from our own, about which we can only speculate and which we can never experimentally confirm.

2. Alternative arguments : UC is already infinite and in many ways all powerful.
   a. The wider universe is infinite. Although most physicists agree that the issue is unsettled, a solid arguments exist in favor of this view (reference xxvii).
   b. There is a purpose to the ongoing creation of universes : to prevent infinity from becoming set and museum-like. Ongoing creation is the means by which infinity continues to be alive. Infinity comes in many renditions, all of which are open-ended : all infinities at any level (technically, at any aleph metric) can keep growing indefinitely.
   c. Mathematics is indivisible. There is no such thing as a partial set of mathematical laws, whereby for example 1+1=2 would hold true but some of its more arcane laws—such as the complex discoveries made by winners of the Fields medal and other pioneers in advanced mathematics—would only progressively arise and develop over time. All of the laws of mathematics, whether known or unknown to humans, instantly flow

seamlessly from the simple statement that 1+1=2. The body of mathematical laws is so extensive, open-ended, infinitely complex and sophisticated that it can only be held within an infinitely advanced mind.

d. What appears to be wanton violence visited upon countless consciousness spikes off the consciousness baseline (*aka* 'souls') embedded in the material universe is the only way, however sad and immensely regrettable, that souls at certain stages of their upward spiritual progress become spurred on to progress and grow towards a more enlightened status. Should they become stuck at some level, as it were ensconced in comfort, the whole universe would then be held back. Wounds and psychic scars will all heal over time, and the soul shall emerge better, tougher, and more mature than before.

e. The principle of mediocrity (*aka* the generalized Copernican principle) militates against our universe being the first, or a very early one, in a possible long string of future universes. It also militates against the universe being unique, which must instead be a constituent part of a wider metaverse containing any number of other universes.

From the above, I would opine that an infinite rather than a rudimentary universal consciousness appears to be more likely.

The 'universe', in the meaning of the putatively intelligent mindstuff behind it, also *seems* to occasionally intervene to allay destinies that seemed inexorably headed for pain and suffering, which may signal intelligence behind it. On such occasions, it seems to act as an unlikely *deus ex machina*, able to stave off looming tragedies, sometimes at the last instant. If we discount such favorable twists of fate as may be ascribed to the statistically unavoidable flukes which will randomly change an event or a long chain of events seemingly ineluctably headed for tragedy, we are still left with a number of puzzling instances of apparent intervention—

such as people caught up in war or in other fateful circumstances escaping tragedy at the last-minute, on a seemingly willful 'intervention of the universe'. Yet, for reasons that appear incomprehensible in the scenario of an intelligent universe, it also fails to intervene on other occasions that would seem to cry out for justified intervention. Some sentient beings, such as innocent animals now incontrovertibly proven to be fully sentient, do not escape the relentlessly tragic fates that life has in store for them from the instant they are born. So many innocent sentient beings, including humans, undergo lives both steeped and ended in terror and suffering that we must ask : if the universe *can* intervene, why then are the oft-horrible destinies that befall so many allowed to happen? Is the mindstuff that underlies the universe capable of intervening for the good? Or, when we believe we spot instances of such interventions, are we but victims of apophenia, of seeing patterns to events where none exist? If the more spiritual scenario laid out in Chapter 2 is closer to the truth of the universe, then there *must* exist incontrovertible, experiential or otherwise, confirmation of instances of its intervention. There should also exist discernible or tentatively credible reasons why it does *not* intervene when it does not, especially in grossly unfair or horrible circumstances.

What gives?

*

If the universe ever intervenes, it could take one of three forms :

1. Extraordinarily unlikely coincidences, taken by many as the result of intervention rather than some statistical fluke or other explainable event. Although all coincidences must be discounted because they can always, albeit sometimes at a stretch, be explained away by the ordinary laws of statistics, they are still worth looking at : we'll still learn something from them, as it will turn out not what we may have expected.

2. Behind-the-scenes interventions, as in serendipitous discoveries or extraordinary dreams resulting in leaps forward, taken to be outcomes of intervention rather than just things that happen.
3. Last but not least, obvious interventions, which in our current mindset (or alternatively our current understanding of the laws of physics) would be seen as some 'supernatural event'.

Coincidences

Extraordinary coincidences just cannot be interpreted as meaningful interventions by the universe : irrespective of how unlikely an event, or even a whole chain of individually unlikely events may be, they can *always* be explained as statistical outliers : it is both extremely unlikely that you, say, win the lottery jackpot, but extremely likely that someone will. Another point is that jaw-dropping coincidences often involve utterly trivial matters, which begs the question of why the universe would bother intervening in trivial matters when so many instances of true tragedy out there would remain so woefully ignored.

Weird coincidences are so prevalent and puzzling that a whole cottage industry has sprung up to try and make sense of them, in a manner more satisfying to our emotions than simply attributing them to cold statistical effects would be. Witness books variously by Dr. Sharon Hewitt Rawlette, a philosopher formerly with Brandeis University, by Dr. David Richo, a psychotherapist who penned *'The Power of Coincidence : How Life Shows Us What We Need to Know'*, and many such in the same vein. Nevertheless, when a coincidence or a chain of unlikely coincidences is just too weird, it might still be explained by a statistical outlier, but there also just might be another explanation, not necessarily involving the universe at large but instead either the phenomenon of *synchronicity*, or alternatively some ill-understood abilities of the mind. The Swiss psychiatrist Carl Gustav Jung surmised synchronicity as an unrecognized property of nature : there would exist a flow of time whereby things or events of a like nature would tend to come together and cluster in time and space, thereby giving rise to the appearance of meaningful coincidences. This view, although not further explained in any deeper sense, probably holds true in certain contexts. For instance, writers Colin Wilson, Arthur Koestler and others have mentioned a special type of 'meaningful coincidence' that seems to repeatedly happen to and help all writers : whenever someone writes a book, coincidences seem to start happening that will assist them in their writing and research. Colin Wilson reports that this effect seems to happen routinely to him and to all of the writers he raised the subject with—to the extent that some authors consider it as a 'due', a normal circumstance in the process of writing that can always be reliably counted on. I am also reminded here of a rather puzzling event that happened to me in my business consulting days, a rather odd if ultimately meaningless case of late-onset synchronicity. I had been consulting for a project with a medium-sized company in Europe and then had moved on. Years later, I am in Melbourne, Australia, where I attend a conference on a business theme loosely related to the business space my erstwhile SME European client operated in. At the drink & meet session after the presentations and talks, someone I did not know and had never seen before came over and for some unfathomable reason buttonholed me for a chat. She started recounting at length how she had just been working in Europe with an SME company, which quickly turned out was my erstwhile client ! I could not get a word in edgeways as she reeled off all their latest news and the latest doings and shenanigans of people I had happened years earlier to know quite well. She had absolutely no idea that I had been directly involved with these very people years before, nor did I tell her. When she was finished, she basically just said her goodbyes and left, leaving me scratching my head and wondering, *what was that*? Did some faint Jungian linkage somehow form from erstwhile immersion in a same business environment, later asserting itself in another place at another time, or was it all just sheer meaningless oddity?

Seemingly extraordinary coincidences are commonplace : Sharon Hewitt Rawlette cites research that shows that in all countries surveyed, about one person in three reports that very odd coincidences played an important part in their lives. Although explainable by statistical outliers, our minds struggle not to assign a deeper meaning to coincidences, if only because some are... well, just beautiful, and some are downright eerie, seemingly involving elements of coincidence across time, both backwards and forwards, and across space. Ernest K. Gann, in his endlessly intriguing 1961 book '*Fate is the Hunter*' in which he chronicles the early years of commercial flight as he saw them from the inside as an airline pilot, describes the incomprehensible coincidences that saved his life, time and again, in an era when the complex interplay of aircraft speed, altitude, weight and many other factors was much less well understood than it now is, and that era's air travel far less safe than is the case today. Psychiatrist Scott Peck, in his famous 1987 book 'The Road Less Traveled', reports that in the vast majority of the hundreds of cases of coincidence happening to his patients, the coincidence turned out to be helpful or very helpful. Because a strong bias towards any extra attribute, such as helpfulness, adds an extra layer of statistical improbability, it further complicates the attribution of some coincidences to mere statistical flukes, and suggests that the whole phenomenon of coincidences might be at least in part richer than mere blind statistics. Information theoretician Vlatko Vedral, whom we encountered earlier, believes synchronicity could be embedded in how information plays out in the world, going so far as surmising that the laws of physics may spring up in the universe at the same time and place as the phenomenon to which they apply. Although this is not a limb we would necessarily care to follow him on, we are nevertheless reminded here of how Jeffrey Kripal, the J. Newton Rayzor Chair in Philosophy and Religious Thought at Rice University, and Dr Anthony Jinks, formerly a professor in neuroscience at the School of Social Sciences and Psychology at the University of Western Sydney, and others have firmly concluded that reality is not material—doing so not on the strength of anything theoretical such as the mathematical considerations laid out earlier in this book, but precisely on the basis of observing how unknown laws of physics seem to occasionally spring up, bring about some weird, unexplainable event, and then disappear again as if dissolving away back into the ether, with the more usual, plain vanilla laws of physics taking over anew and being in charge again.

In some cases of coincidence, mere outlier statistics does not seem to quite fill the bill, and in these cases there must be some other explanation. I will attempt one here below, suggested by two experiences at the far edges of possibility which I lived through, both made up of a long string of interlinked, vanishingly unlikely events.

(Of course, any notion of 'vanishingly unlikely' is subjective, and hunches and gut feelings as to whether some event or circumstance is likely or not can be very misleading. We also are notoriously bad at guesstimating anything that involves numbers—especially big or small numbers, such as may often crop up in probabilities. For instance, the likelihood of two people within any group of people having the same birthday is much higher than we would be apt to think if we're going on instinct rather than on objective calculation. Another, oft-quoted classic example is the likelihood of specifically you breathing in, right now, at the very instant when you are reading these lines, some of the molecules of air that had struck Julius Caesar 's vocal chords when, in his dying breath, he exclaimed 'et tu, Brute!', upon recognizing the presence of his son Brutus among his assassins. A normal gut feeling would be that that would be very unlikely, although impeccable mathematics shows that breathing in a few of these molecules is virtually certain (which becomes readily comprehensible if we realize that there are more molecules of air within a single lungful than there are lungful volumes within the entire Earth atmosphere.) In that spirit, the odds of the individual event links making up the chains of events related below are calculable and confirmed extremely unlikely.

The first such experience goes back a few years, when I was an independent science consultant for corporate clients. One day, returning from a difficult and rather frustrating business trip in Europe, I took a cab from the airport to a hotel I was staying in in Brussels, the European capital. I settled the fare, picked up my briefcase from the back seat and exited the cab. It's only once inside the hotel lift riding up to my room that it suddenly dawned on me that I'd left my other, main suitcase in the cab's trunk. I immediately called the cab dispatching service, but despite their blandishments and promise to call back, it was clear there was nothing they could, or for that matter, would do (I'd rather naively thought they might broadcast a query to the cab fleet. Needless to say, they never did, neither did they ever call back.) I hied back downstairs, hailed a cab in front of the hotel and explained the situation to the cab driver, Mark, letting him know that I was looking for a colleague of his—but I had not much else to go on. Mark started by asking what make was the cab, of which I had no idea, but I did remember the unusual russet hue of the cab's seats. Whereupon he replied there was only *one* cab with that particular interior color in town, but of course he had no idea where the cab would have headed after dropping me off—perhaps some taxi stand somewhere. Where? It's a big city. On a whim, I suggested we drive down to the South Railway Station (one of three main railway stations close to the city center), and off we went. On a quite short segment of road between two turns on the way there, Mark thought he spotted the russet-interior taxi zipping past on the other side, heading the other way. On the off chance that it was factual, we decided to turn around as soon as feasible and changed plans—instead of driving to the taxi stand at the station we'd now try and look for the russet cab at a taxi stand near government offices located farther on, in the general direction of where Mark thought he'd seen the cab going. And there we found it, where the rather flummoxed driver opened his trunk and handed me back my suitcase. The improbable elements here are legion, boarding the only russet interior taxi in town to begin with, boarding a second cab where the driver, who happened to know of the other cab, thought he spotted it going the other way on a very short stretch of road—had we been on that stretch of road a few seconds earlier or later we would have missed it—on a road that we had taken haphazardly to drive, as it turned out, to an irrelevant taxi stand, as the russet cab had no business being on that particular stretch of road if he intended to go to a stand near some government buildings. He must have changed his mind en route as to where he wanted to go to, and finally, guessing the new destination was far from a given, as it could have been any number of other stands, destinations, or picking up some assigned fare. The likelihood of eventually getting back my suitcase would have been small (any other fare could then have simply picked it up.) There was nothing of much value in the case : a change of suits, that kind of thing. It's only on principle that I just didn't want to let it go.

A second, similar case happened a few years later—I'm in Tokyo, where I'm renting a BnB. On the last day of rental I do the routine things—brush teeth, pack bags, and go, leaving the door key behind in the prearranged spot. Later on that day, I am on a suburban train to another destination, with the train line happening to pass through the station nearest to the BnB place I had left earlier that day. A few seconds before the train stops for a brief layover at that station, I happen to glance at my left hand and horror strikes : I had left my gold ring behind at the BnB place ! Probably on the bathroom mirror ledge when brushing my teeth. I scramble to exit the train and hie down a few streets to the BnB place. Once there I just barely catch up with a lady who is just in the process of closing up the place, which she had obviously just been checking on. I point to my finger—and she hands me the ring, visibly relieved that the matter of returning it turns out simpler than it otherwise would have been. Japanese culture is wonderful that way.

Looking back, there is a common thread in these two instances, which I would only recognize in hindsight : I *never doubted for an instant* that I would get my belongings back. The possibility, indeed the overwhelming odds of loss did not register at all on my mental radar : I just thoughtlessly jumped into action, never entertaining the extremely likely outcome that I would not recover my property. Mindlessly, I just got cracking – a course of action which, had I allowed my analytical mind to just come up for air for a brief while, I would not have pursued, as it was just way too unlikely that circumstances of space and time would align towards doing my bidding. But they did. I had intent – strong intent to recover my belongings, no matter what, and somehow the universe obliged...

But, apart from not providing any explanation of the deeper mechanism of how things work, this does not account either for the critical elements which took place *before* the triggering event (i.e., leaving behind the suitcase, or forgetting the ring) that led to the chain of unlikely coincidences. The coincidences began *before* the triggering event : the fact that I happened to board the only 'russet' cab in town (and that to begin with there existed only one russet-interior cab in a town awash with taxis.) Or the fact that I never take off my ring, but for some reason I did on that day (which also explains why picking it back from the bathroom ledge did not cross my mind.)

A number of different explanations can be attempted to explain highly unlikely chains of events, whose constituent events are themselves very unlikely. Extreme statistical outliers is one, and this particular explanation is the only one that explains things 'all the way down', as it makes possible mathematical sense. All other explanations are little more than labels, way stations on the road towards a full understanding which remains elusive : some rendition of synchronicity, or some unexplained or ill-understood power of the mind as I attempted above. More esoteric still would be what is variously called an instance of 'memory of the future', *aka* foreknowledge or precognition : under that view, I never doubted for an instant that I would recover my belongings against mountainous odds *because* somehow I subconsciously knew—in effect remembering from the future that I would. Time works in puzzling ways, as is not only seen in physics in delayed choice experiments and in certain relativistic effects, but also in Roger D. Nelson's above-cited *Global Consciousness Project*. In it, the observed nonrandom spikes off true background random noise, taken to spring from a measure of coherent global consciousness, are routinely observed to begin *before* the corresponding events that will trigger much collective attention and mind focus : as cases in point, nonrandom spikes off the baseline random noise began four hours before the terrorist attacks on 9/11, and a full 24 hours before the Indian Ocean tsunami which killed 230,000 people in December 2004. There are other cases, and nor are Roger Nelson's observations the only ones or the first : in 1966, John Barker, a psychiatrist who was then working in a British mental Hospital, began to investigate whether people who said they had visions of impending disasters could prove helpful in averting them. He got the idea after it emerged that a number of people had independently had visions of the Aberfan disaster in Wales, in which a colliery waste tip slid down a mountain and killed 116 children and 28 adults in a school below. To that end, he set up a 'Premonitions Bureau' telephone line which any member of the public could ring up if they had such visions. Hundreds of people contributed, amongst whom a handful would prove repeatedly able to accurately foresee future calamities and international incidents[xxi].

As ever, seemingly similar situations may result from different causes, or a coming together of causes. In the two narrowly personal cases described above I feel that by somehow jumping into action, by letting the right brain fully take over and totally override whatever the left brain would have admonished, I somehow helped make things align. How exactly is anyone's guess, but a gut feeling makes me doubt if the string of coincidences would otherwise have happened and seamlessly dovetailed to lead to the outcome sought by the more emotional right brain. Perhaps a blend of different causes could also account for whatever elements take place before the triggering event. Unfortunately, such phenomena are neither repeatable nor predictable, and therefore not amenable to lab testing nor mathematical modelling. Understandably, they are therefore shunned as research subjects, and mostly swept under the proverbial rug. It remains that extremely unlikely coincidences have been reported by very many, including Carl Gustav Jung whom we met earlier, Austrian biologist Paul Kammerer, and many others. Paul Broks, a *über*-reductionist neuroscientist who espouses material views, including the view that the neural correlates of consciousness are also its neural originators, reports a string of extraordinary, and extraordinarily unlikely coincidences in his life[xxii]. Anna Broinowski, a Professor at the University of Sydney, recounts in her terrifying memoir 'Datsun Angel' how she was saved from seemingly murderous outback truck drivers, on a stretch of road where a female California hitchhiker had been murdered a week earlier, by a totally unlikely chain of events and coincidences. Elton John once said that he believes he was spared becoming a victim to AIDS, despite his rather freewheeling lifestyle during the eighties, a time when AIDS was out of control and mowing down great artists right and left and far and wide, because he was protected by Life itself, owing to the role he had to play in keeping inspiring young people with his music.

Yet there are also all the counterpoints. 'The Lost Manor', Alain Fournier's first novel, a bittersweet tale of lost love widely hailed as a masterpiece, was also his last : he was killed on the front lines in World War 1. Coincidences can lead to felicitous or life-saving outcomes, and sometimes to tragedy. For example, a remarkably uncanny coincidence helped jumpstart Anthony Hopkins's acting career[xxiii]. At the other end of the range of felicitousness, a research lab I occasionally worked in as a student featured a huge press used for experiments in metallurgy, secured by no fewer than seven independent, differently powered safety devices. One day, when a worker was busy cleaning its surfaces, all seven safeties inexplicably gave way at the same time, killing him on the spot. Or a recently reported case of the ambulance carrying the injured victim of a car crash becoming involved in an accident of its own—the now twice- injured person was then put aboard a new emergency vehicle which then itself promptly crashed—killing its passenger. The cases are countless, on both sides of the ledger, although we would as lief believe psychiatrist Scott Peck's observation that most coincidences turn out to be for the good.

Materialist Brian Klaas, a Professor in politics at University College London, writes that coincidences (which he calls flukes) play the primary role in the way all life unfolds. Coming from his materialist angle whereby a person is nothing more than a mortal and temporary assembly of material atoms and molecules, his view is that coincidences just mindlessly happen, and he reckons that rank flukes play the main role in how the material world unspools. One of the stories he tells is how he came to be born—indeed, in his view, to plain *be*, period—ultimately because of a tragedy that befell his extended family long before he was born. But this worldview seems to fail on solid criteria : first, it is not *rich* and as we have seen, richness (the scenarios of reality that allow vast new realms of possibilities to open up) tends to better describe the rather complex reality out there, and second it ignores the vast body of solid research that suggests that life is much more than just temporary mortal assemblies of inert atoms. It also commits the usual sin of ignoring the smoky part of the dragon—the immaterial yet very real, elephant-in-the-room constant fellow traveler of material reality.

At the other end of the range of opinions and perhaps experiences, Robert Schwartz and others have built a career and a following by investigating how an as-yet discarnate consciousness would plan material-realm experiences before incarnating, with an aim at undergoing specific experiences that will help along its spiritual growth. In doing so, they build on a long tradition : in ancient Greece, Plato tells in his classic 'The Republic' of a man called Er who witnesses the intricately detailed plans that souls make for their forthcoming incarnations on Earth. The concept of earthly lives planned in advance is also rife in a number of cultures world-wide[xxiv]. As such, it would be for instance foreplanned that two people would meet, whereas in our material world such a meeting would appear to be the result of a fluke. Brian Klaas reports the intriguing story of someone who was about to drown in the open sea, but incongruously a ball floated towards him, to which he hung on for dear life, and thereby managed to survive. As it turned out, a couple of boys had been playing ball a few hours earlier on a nearby beach, one had kicked it out to sea and the ball was lost. Some will see it as a mindless fluke, and others will see a measure of intervention.

And as ever, cognitive bias lurks. In his book 'I Can See Clearly Now', Wayne Dwyer looks back at his life and recounts how he can, with the benefit of hindsight, see how Life itself arranged for the necessary people and events to appear in his life at the right times in order to enable and bring about his intended life purpose, engineering a chain of life events (his enrolment in the army, falling ill at just the right time to meet the right circumstances and people, and so on), so that the chain of unfolding events would ensure that he would be inexorably led to the life that he was meant to live. But that does not work. If other events had played out so that he would have ended up becoming a famous footballer instead, he could also pen memoirs laying out how a chain of events in his life unerringly led him to become the famous footballer he would then happen to be. In looking at the wider contexts of life and in exploring unusual possibles, there is the danger of falling into cognitive rabbit holes or falling victim to a measure of magical thinking. The author of otherwise very erudite and intriguing books on unusual experiences once rather puzzlingly put out a text on kairomancy, defined as using random things haphazardly seen in everyday life, such as the first unusual thing one happens to see on the street or such, to inform thoughts and actions. The line between sense and nonsense is sometimes at risk of blurring, and in the absence of better criteria, objective hard science and/or mathematics must surely remain the reliable go-to guides, the ports in all of life's messy storms.

Dreams and Serendipity

The second form is apparent behind-the-scenes interventions, which turn up in the form of extraordinary information imparted to a recipient, often but not always in the form of dreams and vivid dreams : it's August Kekulé discovering the chemical structure of Benzene in a dream, it's Hector Berlioz hearing a 'fabulous symphony' in the exact same dream two nights in a row but remembering only how blissful he felt hearing it (regrettably not the music itself), it's on the other hand Anton Bruckner remembering the music he heard in a dream and scrambling to transcribe it—which would become his symphony Nb. 7 in E major, widely deemed his masterpiece yet according to him never achieving the beauty of what he had heard, it's Paul McCartney dreaming his iconic song 'Yesterday' and Keith Richards dreaming up what would become the celebrated anthem of the 60's, '*Satisfaction*' by The Rolling Stones, it's Samuel Taylor Coleridge remembering 300 lines of a poem he dreamt, scrambling to write them down—but upon being interrupted at line 54 promptly forgetting all of the rest (the remaining 54-line poem becoming what is now known as the 'Kubla Khan'), and, most intriguing of all, it is Srinivasa Ramanujan's complex mathematical dreams which contributed to advancing higher mathematics, although he had zero formal mathematical training, and it's also the many essential discoveries in medicine and other fields that came about by extraordinary serendipity.

Supernatural?

Which brings us to the third possible kind of intervention : 'Supernatural' forms of intervention, rare yet widely reported, such as described in '*Hasidic Tales of the Holocaust*'[xxv], or as in the reports of

'The Angel of Mons' in World War 1, or even the apparitions at Fatima, and many such other cases. There are two issues with trying to make sense out of this third form of intervention : first, they are hardly repeatable and hence can only ever speak to the very limited number of people who either witnessed or were affected by them (on very rare occasions they are partly repeatable, as was the case at Fatima, because the dates of subsequent apparition events had been foretold.) Second, such claims are wide open to fraud—and it is inherently difficult to winnow out the few possibly truthful reports from the vast ruck of fraudulent ones.

Adding to the confusion, the very concept of 'supernatural' is moot. Physics is still a work in progress, and the boundaries of what constitutes natural phenomena falling within the known laws of physics, as opposed to supernatural, are pushed back all the time. There are many rather trivial cases of events that appear to be supernatural, including many of those reported by Anthony Jinks, Jeffrey Kripal, Michael Nahm and others—all of which are open to different interpretations, but which at the very least seem to confirm what we already know : reality is not material, at least not in the way it has traditionally been taken to be, as most of the dragon is smoky. Many people and most families have a personal or family tale of something inexplicable that happened to them. Such cases do not necessarily imply agency or meaningfulness, but only confirm *experimentally* what the mathematics says on paper, that life isn't material. Anthony Jinks is one of the few who have extensively studied extremely odd phenomena that seem to routinely happen in everyday life to thousands of people. Despite attempting *possible* cogent explanations-tentatively reasonable explanations for seemingly unreasonable events, including the possibility that information theoretician Vlatko Vedral is right and that novel, hitherto unknown physical laws sometimes spring up at the same instant as the events they govern, Tony Jinks was never able to settle on one clincher explanation, leaving open the possibility that different causes are involved in different instances of phenomena which otherwise may appear very similar or identical. Be that as it may, most of the alternative possible explanations to these puzzling events involve the more conscious aspects that underlie our material universe. Other researchers have broached such studies–Mary Barrington, Stephen Braud, and others, but because the subject matter is odd to the point of being uncomfortable, no such studies have ever become mainstream, or even widely known. Yet, should anyone look back at their lives, they might well find instances of odd, inexplicable events. Dr. Tania Luhrmann, the Watkins University Professor in the Stanford Anthropology Department, cites a number of such cases, and then observes that most people, when experiencing such odd events, will puzzle for a while, and then mostly just forget about it and move on. The inexplicable event may be of either minor or, much less often, major significance and consequence—a wink and nudge from the universe, as it were, but so far beyond the range of our everyday reference frames that it is dismissed as 'one of those things', whose memory soon fades into oblivion.

There also exist intriguing hints to the permanence of spirit. Unfortunately, after-life (and before-life) studies inevitably attract frauds, which discredits the whole field as a serious scientific pursuit before it can even establish itself. Yet there are also the rare few with impeccable credentials and personal histories, such as Raymond Moody, who cannot just be dismissed out of hand. There are also those who publicly perform extraordinary works that would be quite hard to emulate, typically when in a trance, such as the Brazilian trance painter Luiz Gasparetto, who displays extraordinary abilities that resist simple explanations, as he seems to temporarily seamlessly 'channel' and deploy the unique abilities and the unmistakable signature styles of deceased famous painters. (Of course, such abilities could somehow spring from the alleged channelers' own brains, although exactly *how* would likely prove as difficult to explain as would any other explanation : there is just no simple answer to such phenomena, which is also why they are not seriously researched nor well-known.)

There are published reports and books by people who claim to have been in touch with the spirits of dead celebrities. None of those I have happened to riffle through seemed overly credible (with the possible exception of Wendy Weir 's report on her conversations with the 'soul' of Grateful Dead frontman Jerry Garcia after his death. In her case, there is no suspicion of fraud, yet what she perceived as Jerry Garcia's words may have sprung from a variety of sources, including, of course, her own subconscious), and a few were obvious, threadbare, ultimately immensely sad fabrications.

Because any other people's more unusual experiences are both private and unverifiable and therefore automatically suspect, the only way anybody can touch the numinous is through their direct own. I once had an interesting dream involving John Lennon, decades after his death in 1980. He had passed early, at a time when he probably still had much to contribute. The dream was both very vivid and in its wider context oddly *logical*, as follows.

Like the rest of us, John Lennon went through phases in his life—which included periods of heaviness and angst, as well as lightness and joy. Heaviness and angst suffused his first solo album, 'Plastic Ono Band' released in 1970. The album opens with 'Mother', a track ushered by ominous, slow, heavy bell chimes reflecting the number's angst. In counterpoint, he later deliberately used a bell intro again on 'Just Like Starting Over', the opening track to his 1980 'Double Fantasy' album. As he later told an interviewer, he had by then resolved the dire angst that had infused the 'Plastic Ono Band' album and, now in a far happier place, he was signaling it by using light and joyful crystalline bell chimes on 'Starting Over', referencing, and at the same time bringing closure to, the earlier tones.

On the angst-ridden 'Plastic Ono Band' album, there is another track, 'God', where he repeatedly sings mantra-like, no less than 15 times, *'I don't believe in'*, followed by the names of things or people he does not, or did not, believe in at the time of singing :

> I don't believe in magic
> I don't believe in I-ching
> I don't believe in Bible
> I don't believe in Tarot
> I don't believe in Hitler
> I don't believe in Jesus
> I don't believe in Kennedy
> I don't believe in Buddha
> I don't believe in Mantra
> I don't believe in Gita
> I don't believe in Yoga
> I don't believe in Kings
> I don't believe in Elvis
> I don't believe in Zimmerman
> I don't believe in the Beatles

And this is where my odd vivid dream experience fit right in : I saw and heard John singing a new song called *'I believe'*, its tune loosely halfway between the new Beatles song *'Now and Then'* (released months after the dream, which it therefore cannot have influenced), and singer Rory Charles Graham (*aka* Bones and Rags Man)'s number *'Skin'*—with John happily listing things he believes in, in part gainsaying some of his previous lyrics, the sound definitely his, and, just as he had done with the track *'Mother'* referencing his later track *'Just Like Starting Over'*, referencing in the number I dreamt *'I Believe'* his earlier, darker *'God'* song. Needless to say, I can never know how this dream came about or where it took its source—all the same, I am glad I heard it.

7 Destiny and Tragedy

If, in keeping with the above view of a non-rudimentary, intelligent universal consciousness, we assume that the universe *can* intervene in the affairs of humans and sentient beings, then the question arises as to why the lives and destinies of so many on Earth are so imbued with tragedy, why does not the Universe intervene more often if it can. So many innocent sentient beings undergo lives steeped and ended in terror and suffering that we are left to wonder, if the universe can intervene, why then are the oft-horrible destinies that befall so many allowed to happen, how does brutal suffering make any sense in the wider scheme of things, and if it somehow does, is it commensurate with its intended purpose. Humans do suffer through war, disease, loss of livelihood and many other ordeals, and the grossly unfair destinies which can be seen everywhere, all the time, conjure up a grim sense of unspeakable injustice : some newborn is born to the world in a place which just became engulfed in a merciless war, and is killed together with her mom in a bombing, another one is left by his parents to slowly suffocate in a locked car in the sun, an innocent suffers a miscarriage of justice and is sent to jail for life, someone falls ill at a young age and goes through painful months before she dies. There are endless instances of tragic fates out there, and out of the plethora we can pick out many. One, out of billions : British war surgeon David Nott, in his haunting report from the front lines of the 2012 Syrian war, describes an "incandescently beautiful" girl of about 13 years of age brought badly wounded to his field hospital, looking with beautiful, hauntingly intelligent and defiant eyes at the world that the adults had made for her… and she then promptly died[xxvi]. For some, it starts at birth : the worldwide statistics of terrible and often lethal innocent child abuse is horrendous. Even in relatively affluent and comfortable Western societies, such as the UK, Germany, France, the USA, Italy and so on, the statistical numbers are pretty consistent : Month in month out, one young child dies at the hands of their parents and/or caretakers per five million inhabitants. In other words, in a country with about 60 million inhabitants, such as Italy or the UK, 12 young children die at the hands of their parents or other caretakers *every month*. In the US with its 350 million inhabitants, the figure rises to 70 children a month. Of course, in terms of destinies, it's but the visible, deathly tip of the iceberg : it is estimated that one person in five has suffered medium to severe abuse in their childhood. The examples are manifold and endless—how does it make any sense?

If a single, more or less intelligent consciousness pervades the universe, should it not be capable of occasionally intervening in what would then be its own internal affairs—at least whenever the level of hurt visited upon sentient beings exceeds an incomprehensible threshold of pain? Why and how is there so much suffering, and so many destinies prove so gruesome? What possible justifiable purpose does it serve—whether collective, individual, whether over the short haul or in the fullness of time? A simple and possibly desirable answer would be that it's just the way it is, and that's that, but that cannot be a legitimate answer, because there is more to the universe than mere blithe mindlessness, and explore alternative explanations we then must. Some may try to explain away dire life circumstances by resorting to various esoteric explanations, such as a loaded karma or other such. Be that as it may, all of these explanations would utterly fail where animals are concerned, and they therefore can never be entirely valid. Yet many humans live happy and meaningful lives. Not so with animals : the vast majority of innocent animals, incontrovertibly proven to be fully sentient, cannot escape the relentlessly tragic fates that life has in store for them from the instant they are born.

Science has only rather recently been playing catch-up with what pet owners have long known, to wit that pets and other animals are very far from being mere biological robots. A growing body of science convincingly shows that *all* animals are far more sentient and aware than was once thought. To any pet owner, it seems obvious that pets are *persons*, albeit not human persons, with their own personalities, their own way of apprehending and dealing with their reality and events in the world. Feelings that are quite recognizable from a human standpoint are often observed, never mind the dire warnings of scientists to beware of anthropomorphism : jealousy, contentment, trust or distrust, and at times a quite surprising ability to cope with unexpected events which their instincts cannot possibly have prepared them for, are all routinely on display. As it turns out, the science is firmly on the side of the existence of individual sentience in virtually all animals, including insects as we saw earlier. The sentience of animals differs from the sentience of humans both by the intensity, or 'height' of the spike of consciousness off the universal baseline they represent, and by the *nature* and quality of that spike (or in other words, the multidimensional *shape* of that spike.) For instance, grown-up horses seem to sometimes behave as if they were 5 year old humans, which, translated in spike-of-consciousness terms suggests that a horse's spike may have roughly the same height against the baseline consciousness background as a five year old human (although a markedly different shape within the multidimensional space representing various attributes and criteria), an analogy of scary relevance when we consider the treatment and destinies meted out to most farm animals. A staggering 72 billion—that's billions, not millions—land animals are slaughtered every year worldwide for food. If we include birds, it's 200 billion farm animals that are killed every year, and there are a further one trillion fish and sea animals—of which we now know that they are also sentient and in some cases demonstrably intelligent[xxvii]. Because of the overwhelming economic pressures of feeding 8 billion-odd people at the least possible cost, the conveyor belt-like process of slaughtering animals takes in stride many inefficiencies and errors which would be too costly to fix, and many animals pay the price in staggering suffering–pigs boiled alive, cattle sliced alive, and the like, all things that have been exhaustively documented in a raft of books and articles dealing with conditions in the killing floors of slaughterhouses, by both journalists and former slaughterhouse employees[xxviii].

How can this make any sense is what we must turn to next.

8 Redeeming Sense?

The consciousness of *any* sentient being on Earth is made up of two separate components : an individual or *private* part (which we'll designate by A), and a collective part, B, sometimes described as an element of 'hive consciousness'. The hive consciousness element B is made up of a part still tightly enmeshed with the ever-present consciousness baseline that still exists within someone's overall consciousness, whereas the balance of that being's consciousness is made up by the more spike-like, individual component A. In insects such as ants and bees, B is dominant to the point of probably being almost the only element of consciousness, whereas at the other end of the scale, in humans, it is vestigial—although definitely present, as evidenced by the studies of above-cited Howard Bloom, Roger Nelson, John Barker, and others.

The question of whether inescapable suffering in sentient individuals' lives makes any redeeming sense, therefore splits up into two distinct questions : does suffering makes sense in the context of A, and somehow serves to enhance in some way the private component of the consciousness of an individual? Or does it rather make more sense in the context of B, and somehow impacts and presumably helps collective consciousness, either across a given species or across the board of all consciousnesses? As the case may be, could it somehow help both A and B—or neither?

There is little doubt that the suffering of one species can just be the unnecessary and unwelcome side effect of something that happens to be useful to another species, as is the case in the meat industry. Horrible as it is for prey, there is no doubt that eating meat helps predators. Making use of whatever organisms can be found in one's immediate vicinity is what jump started the transition from unicellular to multicellular lifeforms, and modern predation is a direct descendant of the exploitation by primitive organisms of any available resources in their immediate surroundings (a process well described at popular science level in e.g. Peter Godfrey-Smith's extraordinary book '*Other Minds : The Octopus and the Evolution of Intelligent Life*'.) Closer to our era, it is very likely that the cognitive abilities of early hominids and humans were enhanced by the eating of meat[xxix]. Shockingly enough though, the suffering may also sometimes be an end in itself—as in bullfighting or fox hunting, still used for entertainment in some cultures, or as in staged public executions, thankfully now mostly confined to the ash heap of regrettable history.

Life, writ large, seeks to blossom into every available niche, irrespective of the price to other preexisting life forms. It seems that if there is any redeeming value attached to predation, it lies in maximizing overall, wider life, no matter what, irrespective of any individual-level cost. Thus, predators appear whenever some biological niche opens : a Danish experiment looked at how the bacterial fauna that lives in our mouths would develop if left unchecked. To do so, the experiment dispensed with oral hygiene in the volunteers who bravely participated in the experiment. They were paid to not brush their teeth, and the Danish dentists monitoring the experiment soon observed new, never-seen-before species of bacteria, including a new aggressive predator species that sprang up within weeks to feed on the more usual bacteria known to populate ill-maintained mouths, which were by then lushly thriving in the controlled conditions of the experiment.

It is indisputable that some amount of suffering leads to life raising its game across the board, not simply because it leads to a wider and more varied availability and distribution of nutrients (across the board, since predator scat also fertilizes the soil that grows their prey's food), but also because both predator and prey species must remain mentally sharp to survive, becoming steadily more observant and physically fit in the arms race to survive. Prey species substantially benefit cognitively from predation, since they need to stay fit, escape, and above all keep adapting. Animal species in the wild, such as neat (i.e., buffaloes and cattle) or dogs, unprotected by farmers and unshielded from predators, have been shown to be smarter against a set of simple criteria than their domestic counterparts. For farm animals which today make up the vast majority of several species of land animals, the steady downgrading of the cognition abilities they once needed to survive seems to be the rule. Today's industrial-scale factory farms further worsen the cognitive abilities of millions of animals bereft of stimuli and challenges. Zoos nowadays routinely address the issue, because their animals are apt to go unstable if faced with no challenges at all : for instance, food may be placed slightly out of reach so that animals such as giraffes and others must figure out ways to access it, thereby exercising mental abilities. Farm animals' end of life session at the slaughterhouse seems to have no redeeming value for them, so that any redeeming value seems strictly other species'—such as that of consumers of meat. In a similar line of thought, Michael Lewis observes in his book 'Boomerang' that before the 2008 global financial crisis hit, Iceland had become a society that "turned killing fish into Ph.D.'s", meaning that the proceeds from its extensive fishing industry fueled an economic capability that allowed many Icelanders to pursue higher academic studies both at home and abroad—thereby contributing to raising the overall level of cognition, not only narrowly in Iceland but in the world at large and indeed, the universe itself. In the context of all sentient beings being embodied spikes of consciousness—incarnate '*souls*' for short—with no choice but to grow in spirituality and wisdom, another view has been put forward by people whose worldviews are informed by Eastern philosophies : some animal souls, at some early point in their *samsara*—their cycle of births and reincarnation in some form—are apt to become stuck in a comfortable incarnate place, a spiritual dead end where they simply enjoy being 'in the flesh' and no longer feel the urge to strive towards more spirituality—which however the universe wants and needs them to do. The woes that then befall their physical bodies jars them out of the snug comfort zone they would otherwise risk associating with being in the flesh, and cause a trauma that will carry over several incarnations and force them to no longer rely on the body for happiness and comfort. Under this view, the brutality of some destinies would be a direct consequence of the ability to become stuck in some evolution rut, rather than always striving to keep evolving. Perhaps a faint seed of free will is embedded in every consciousness, and every consciousness or iota of consciousness arising off the baseline carries such a seed—and as the now individual iota of consciousness slowly grows into a spike, the potential ruts on its way up are many, out of which Life wants that it be jarred. Should that view be wrong and a faint seed of free will not even be there, then getting stuck in an evolutionary rut would not result from the willful agency of any consciousness, and the brutality of many fates would then remain as unspeakable as it appears to be.

Reverting to humans, the historical importance of war in accelerating human progress has also been noted. In his jarring 2000 Book '*War : What Is It Good For?*', Yale scholar Ian Morris examines the benefits that have historically flowed from the armed conflicts that have beset the human race since time immemorial. At the very least, war has considerably sped up technological and scientific progress. More significantly, it has also forced substantial progress in the *mindsets* of societies : for example, a strong case can be made that ossified attitudes in regards to social classes and the role of women in society have only been overcome in many countries because of the disruptions wrought by World War 1, and that the explosion of popular creativity and culture that took place in the sixties was largely traceable to a generation that was coming of age at a time when all of the old landmarks had disappeared, amidst the chaos and deprivations caused by World War2 and its immediate aftermath. Wars cause sharp wrenchings, which become inflection points best described by Einstein's aphorism that new solutions can only flow from new mindsets, most efficiently brought about by the destruction of the old. Yet the price paid in human wars is inordinate—a lesson that some people hailing from post-war generations seem to have to learn ever anew, as soon as their parent's generation no longer have dreadful first-hand war tales to report to their children.

Through 'life raising its game', aggregate world consciousness becomes over time sharper, smarter, and more intense, and the faint consciousness baseline that pervades the universe gradually lifts whole, with the spikes that are people and other sentient beings all becoming ever steadily higher. From our standpoint rather than that of the universe itself, a possible objection would be that raising life's game is a value judgment, therefore not necessarily valid. Yet, looking back at human history, we have little choice but to conclude that raising cognitive ability is the more valid alternative, and that it has always been urgent : there are just too many examples of behaviors, once deemed normal and accepted as such by everyone, which were horrendously, often criminally stupid—torture to the death meted out in many societies for what is now quite justifiably seen as peccadilloes, for example, or conveyor-belt sacrificing of youths so that the sun will deign to rise again in the morning, and the like. Human IQs have thankfully steadily grown, ever since the concept of intelligence quotient got its start, and statistical assessments began. Its 100 median value is revised upwards every few years, tracing, so far, a steady rise. If the game of the universe is then to 'raise its game', then predation in its many forms, from preyed-upon deep sea worms through our mechanized meat industry to wars, seems to serve the purpose.

But could not a 'raising of the game' be achieved by other means? It is also a moral question. In acknowledging the presence of a sole consciousness underlying the universe, we have imbued it with meaning, rescued it from cold materialistic meaninglessness and opened it up to purpose. Yet somehow, we seem to have arrived at a place which may in some ways be worse than meaninglessness, a place where innocent, terrified sentient beings are routinely hurt beyond any rhyme or reason, although something could actually be done to prevent it. Keenly aware of the dilemma, many have sought to lend meaning to the unacceptable and unfathomable, to battered children, Holocaust victims, young people killed in old men's wars, and all the sorry litany. Trawling through the available literature on the subject, we variously encounter a patient under hypnosis who tells his reincarnation therapist that he will reincarnate as a child into famine-stricken area to 'learn the compassion he failed to learn in this life', a rape victim telling that she raped someone as a man in a previous life and now must pay retribution, someone born into horrible conditions whose prior incarnations had been exemplary and for whom it 'had been decided' that they needed to be 'tested' to ascertain where their limits of goodness lay, and so forth. Rabbi Yonassan Gershom cites people in regression therapy not only 'remembering' their prior lives as Holocaust victims but also still earlier lives that could explain their subsequent choice of a lifetime as a victim, thereby settling karmic debts they had incurred by accepting a life on the other side of the divide. Whereas all these stories are intriguing within the context of an intelligent universe, none are of course anywhere near proven.

Yet, there must also exist *other* roads to wisdom, spiritual growth, and enhanced cognition. People can learn by example rather than by coercion. Many studies show, for example, that the children who do best at school are emphatically not those who are yelled at or coerced by their parents, but those whose parents set an example at home[xxx]. On the more esoteric side, many people come back as better persons from near death experiences, because they perceived that the experience ushered them into the presence of highly evolved beings who showed an example of what can be, or they felt they met with exceptional love. In the same vein, feral or street animals such as cats or dogs mellow down over time after they are rescued and treated well, and typically gradually become trusting and comfortable again in the presence of humans. The question thus arises as to what gain exactly is ever achieved by going through a brutal or brutalizing phase. Is there essential spiritual value in going through a vast range of phases and experiences of all kinds as we rise up in consciousness and wisdom? In her memoirs, Dolores French, an erstwhile willing professional prostitute, insists that in her experience Quote prostitutes are tougher and smarter than other women Unquote. That may well be part of an overall wider, deeper-time story, but Marie Curie or Rosa Parks and countless others would conceivably beg to differ. In a universe craving upwards evolution, the roads to some form of rising spiritual awakening must be manifold.

The question of how the widespread preponderance of hurt in this universe can be justified can be analyzed in cold engineering terms from the standpoint of efficiency and of results achieved : the universe—*this* universe, with no speculation as to the possible existence of other universes—has an expiry date. It will end, one way or another, in about 100 billion years. By then, which mechanism aiming at 'lifting its game' will have raised the most the qualities deemed as desirable by a conscious universe, by the part that endures after all of its material expression has expired? In our physical world, there is no question that war and predation and competition and other forms of brutal pressure contribute to lifting the intensity of all-around smarts, awareness, and other desirable qualities. Mundane examples from everyday life at lesser intensity levels than war or predation also corroborate this view : for example, students cramming late into the night for their exams would probably not put in the same efforts and/or occasional all-nighters if they weren't afraid of flunking, and instead of staying home and studying on a Saturday night, they would likely much rather throw a party with friends : anyone who has ever been on a campus will confirm that those who party too much do less well that those who worry more and cram, and fail more often. For animals, the pressure of predation, and of any other difficulties such as having to deal with limited resources, forces them devise strategies of survival—and smarten up. But if learning by example or even by kindness works for at least some humans, could it possibly work as well as, or even better than suffering, and achieve the same quality of results?

The question is twofold : if there is a measurable or even significant difference between those two ways of learning and raising one's game, could not the difference be closed by some other means than brutality, such as expending more time or some other way? And, if the more brutal way indeed leads to better outcomes, does the difference justify all the pain and harsh fates, including all the pain that has not yet taken place but which will already inexorably befall billions of sentient beings over the foreseeable future (say, the next few centuries)? If all it takes to bring about a similar or the same level of higher consciousness is more *time*, even if spread out into deep time or even into the 'Cycles of Time' mooted by Roger Penrose and others beyond the lifetime of our current universe[xxxi], then it surely would be worthwhile to not brutalize anyone and just let more time—more cosmic time—work its wonders.

But because rising individual peaks of consciousness contribute to the upwards evolution of overall consciousness, there is the issue of how highly evolved consciousness can become, of whether there is a cap or ceiling to achieved evolution (against which set of criteria needs not concern us at this stage) and if so, how best can it be further lifted. If simply more time is allowed for the purpose of enhancing overall consciousness, the question arises as to whether the *same* top level of consciousness be attained, in any fullness of time, by means of kindness as it can with suffering? If, even in infinite time, a higher level of consciousness can *only* be reached through a measure of suffering, then the universe as we know it could be justified. It would constitute a spiritual justification for all the suffering we witness.

Perhaps the answer is not ours to know.

Many have sought for an answer. For what it's worth, a very different view from the above was put forward by unconventional therapist and psychologist Dr. Thomas Zinser—an intriguingly unsettling possibility, neatly illustrating anew how wildly different theories can fit the same real-world observations and facts. A psychotherapist, Thomas Zinser built his successful psychological therapy practice by sourcing advice from what he perceived as a disincarnate being whom he called 'Gerod' (how he came to this unconventional MO, and what his statistics of success were, are exhaustively told in his 2011 book 'Soul-Centered Healing'.) The proof of the pudding being in its eating, a measure of whether Dr. Zinser was justified in using this extremely unconventional source of therapeutic insights is whether it worked : it did. (Of course, history amply proves that the fact that something works well does not necessarily bear any relationship to its factualness : for instance, the imperative of survival has led in humans to countless instances of severe cognitive bias, which helped us survive but never to properly understand the world, often on the contrary.)

As it turned out, "Gerod" offered a view of the genesis of our universe rather perfectly contradictory to the usual view held by most, and especially by most religions. Most religions use a variation on the theme of 'God created the universe' (irrespective of whether God created the universe through the Big Bang 13.5 billion years ago, or in some other way.) Gerod's assertion is that it is the forces of *darkness* instead—something like the devil—who created this universe, a universe bogged down in coarse matter as opposed to the far more subtle and spiritual realms that constitute the invisible rest of the metaverse. Which would explain why lifting both the whole baseline and individuals is so essential, and why we hail from origins plagued with ignorance, disease and mayhem, far more horrible than a present which in turn is slowly evolving into an ever better future. Under that picture, the reason why the "universe" does not intervene for the better good so often would be that it *can't* : what could intervene would be the subtler realms of the metaverse, only able to break through to the molasses of this coarser universe sparingly and with much effort—a bit like onlookers at a bicycle race can only provide water to but a few of the racers, and not much else. Thomas Zinser's tentative explanation is only one of several that may be resorted to in order to explain the pain and suffering that we witness in our short lives in the material universe. Others, such as Robert Moss and others, have offered other speculations—such as scenarios involving sundered, broken fragments of souls, afoot in the universe and sometimes incarnating haphazardly and temporarily into the material world.

Recapping briefly where we are : because ours is a mathematical universe, the likeliest description of how the universe came to be is through the mathematics enabled by a prior underlying consciousness, the 'universal consciousness'. This universal consciousness is reflected in a low baseline consciousness seen to pervade the material universe. The pervading universal consciousness (UC) is most likely an already immensely evolved apex consciousness, to the point that at least some of its attributes are infinite—in effect godlike, in the old meaning of that word. Yet, because infinity can always grow further, and because it must always grow further in order to stay alive, its work of further growth is never done.

*

Yet, even if we accept the scenario whereby a measure of hurt is not only unavoidable but even desirable, it does not ensue that we are duty bound to accept its major item of awful baggage : the role of predation as the dominant accelerator of evolution. We are always free to choose. No power can force us to accept anything, especially something as woefully undignified as predation.

In any event, we seem to only have ourselves to count on. If we are dim enough to want to torture people, to burn animals alive, and to wage devastating wars for ridiculous peccadilloes, no one will prevent us. It is time to look at what future we may be creating for ourselves—should we be smart enough already to not destroy the planet.

9 Raising the Bar of Embodied Consciousness

Under both the materialistic and the spiritual scenarios, the universe has no choice but to keep complexifying in order to better dissipate the free energy in its midst, as is mandated by the laws of mathematics it conforms to. It most effectively does so through the ongoing complexification of all the *life forms* in its midst. The key difference between the two scenarios laid out in Chapters 1 and 2 lies in that in the former case, complexification exclusively benefits the evolving universe : life forms spring up from nowhere, serve out their purpose, and then vanish back into nothingness. The formerly blind and inert universe may then ultimately complexify enough to develop some kind of temporary sentience, thereby significantly speeding up its dissipation of free energy.

In the second scenario, complexification benefits instead the individual life forms themselves, with the universe being then the vehicle by which life forms improve themselves towards a more refined state of being. In this scenario, there will surely come a time when some person has so much 'grown in wisdom' that she can no longer grow much further by the sole agency of its experiencing a material universe, because its available material toolset has now become too coarse for the purpose of further progressing an already highly evolved person. Yet the ever-resourceful universe is devising ways whereby the available tools to its ends become ever more sophisticated, not only by means of evolution, but also through the shorter term agency of the resourcefulness of its apex life forms. Specifically, does the current push towards *transhumanism*, the enhancement of human bodies beyond mere biology, only benefits the materialistic scenario, as some believe, or is there also a 'spiritual' case for it?

Throughout history, humankind has looked for ways to artificially enhance the range and intensity of the experiences life on

Earth can provide, by whatever means time and place have allowed : the drugs of the shaman, the rituals and music of earlier societies designed to beget states of altered and enhanced consciousness, and so on. In the modern age, new technologies keep being added to the assortment of available means—such as, variously, the binaural sound waves developed by Heinrich Wilhelm Dove and used at the Monroe Institute, or modern advances in biochemistry—fueling an explosion in the available capabilities, and opening doors to experiences well beyond what limited traditional means could offer—witness Steven Kotler's progress report in his 2019 book 'Stealing Fire', or Michael Pollan's 2020 'How to Change Your Mind'.

Concurrently, developments in Artificial Intelligence (AI) designed to assist and enhance our lives are expanding beyond anyone's ability to keep track. Driven by economic imperatives, AI is becoming all the buzz. A ceaseless flood of new developments, capabilities and potentially new areas of application leave little room to foresee or even understand where it is all going. Max Tegmark's noteworthy 2017 book on the theme, 'Life 3.0', is one welcome attempt to take stock. Perhaps by design, the many interviews on the subject of professionals at the forefronts of developments typically end up begging far more questions than they put to rest.

AI is aiding the development of *transhumanism*, which will also include significant material enhancements to the human body itself, whereas the more traditional means of experiential enhancement typically used to rely on and use our bodies *as they are*. In the not so distant future, many of our inherited biological body elements could become replaceable by engineered parts, capable of achieving superior performance, and of creating wholly new abilities, thus making some of our biological heritage obsolete. As compelling societal and economic reasons combine to make the development towards widespread AI and a measure of transhumanism ineluctable, at the current pace of progress and change, we might end up morphing at some point into a new species, with increasingly tenuous links to our earlier selves. We may be on the road towards becoming *hybrids* through augmented bodies—cast further and further adrift from who we once were. These new capabilities, well beyond anything we have witnessed before, bear the risk—or, depending upon viewpoint, hold out the opportunity—to change us beyond what so far has made up our human essence, our very humanity.

From a spiritual angle, is such a development for the *good,* or the *bad,* or could it be just neutral? To answer, we first need to decide what it is that we are doing on Earth in the first place, what our purpose (if any), or rather our eschatology—our end purpose—is. Why we are here at all can hardly be objectively settled, and different people with different mindsets and/or life experiences will favor different answers. A traditional materialist, hewing to a view that all existence stems from random chemical forces and processes temporarily arising within a meaningless material universe, will answer that there is no reason whatsoever to our existence. At the other end of the scale, a traditional religious type may come up with reasons serving whatever pre-formatted spirituality he or she may cleave to.

Many will probably agree that the purely individual purpose of Earth-bound human existence is to *learn, learn, learn* and then learn some more. In the exquisite phrasing of an old European adage, the purpose of our passage on Earth is to *not die a nitwit*—to learn as much as possible within our imparted time. To achieve this, life must expose us to as many learning experiences and situations as possible. Many will also believe, with ample justification, that the purpose of life is ultimately to love, to learn how to love. Learning to love, or to deploy love, however, already presupposes a level of sophistication and/or enlightenment that may not yet attained by all, and to get to that level one surely must first be exposed to all kinds of experiences from a range of angles, across a wide and varied board. Planet Earth seems to operate as a processing machine whose purpose is to elevate life forms (first and foremost ours) and ready them for better, more subtle futures.

The sum total of possible *novel*, contributory experiences on planet Earth is of course limited to whatever the Earth environment is able to put on offer. Should a person, or a group of people, reach an uncommonly advanced level of enlightenment, then their further presence within the Earth environment would soon hit the law of diminishing returns, and become a waste of time for their overarching purpose of learning. Not that Earth would necessarily have a limited potential for new experiences, but from a certain level of sophistication new experiences would not be *novel* enough to contribute much to the purpose of learning. To take a simple example, say that you have learnt a few languages, and thereby learnt how to perceive things from a variety of disparate cultural viewpoints and angles. Soon, learning any further languages will turn into an exercise of been there, done that, and what else is new? Doing so would still be new, but no longer novel.

East and West traditionally see upwards human evolution in different lights – the East emphasizing individual learning through reincarnation cycles which ultimately become no longer needed and cease occurring, whereas the West sees evolution more in terms of a collective process, whereby societies become more and more intelligent, tolerant and yes, *loving* with each generation – irrespective of whatever temporary local setbacks may occur.

How can transhumanism serve the purpose of learning?

Meet Jane, a traditional, biological human who has become highly evolved. She has learnt all that is humanly possible within her lifetime and has reached an enviable level of enlightenment, which would make any further experience on Earth or similar a life of newness but not of novelty – boring and non-contributive. There would be little reason for people such as Jane to go through, say, a continued presence or another lifetime on a place such as Earth : instead of gathering further progress, the person – the soul – involved would then slow down and pause, go through a period of not much further progress and even possibly backslide (whether under Eastern or Western terms is immaterial here.) Whither Jane? The consciousness that in her Earth-bound lifetime was Jane lives on. Without the availability of new capabilities afforded by transhumanism, her further evolution would have to take place somewhere else to keep pace—in other, more subtle realms than our coarse material world, possibly somewhere within the more subtle realms described by the likes of Jürgen Ziewe, Robert Moss, and many others. Yet, by enhancing the ability to continue to learn from within a material environment, transhumanism, when fully developed and available, could push back the boundary where Earth-bound experiences fall short and become inadequate in terms of serving the key purpose of learning.

Whether it's for the good or bad would then depend on one's viewpoint : some people on their deathbeds are relieved to finally be able to go and leave behind this world perceived as mad and coarse, eager to never ever again have anything to do with it—no matter how possibly improved and enhanced. Others mentally drag and kick and 'rage, rage against the dying of the light' (*as per* Dylan Thomas), striving with all their might to stick around within the material world they perceive as their natural home.

Jeffrey Kripal has penned a number of books where he examines life at the upper reaches of human evolution on Earth, and how these upper boundaries may be lifted. From his extraordinary 2022 book 'The Superhumanities', two major takeaways can be drawn. The first one is that *reality is not material*, a case he importantly makes, as mentioned earlier, not from a science but from an experiential angle—from observations of how our familiar reality sometimes utterly breaks down without warning—phenomena that have also been independently observed by a slew of other Academics and authors (such as Tony Jinks, and others—who corroborate the extraordinary observations Prof. Kripal cites in support of reality not being material.) The second key takeaway is the compelling case Jeffrey Kripal makes that, unbeknownst to most, humans all possess *extraordinary* latent abilities, which will easily come to the fore if only they're cultivated a bit, and that the very essence of who we are lies squarely in those abilities rather than in the more superficial markers we usually view as indicative of selfhood and identity. He makes this case primarily from an experiential approach, leavened with theoretical and philosophical considerations.

We must wonder what's next for anyone who would have reached a level of evolution whereby they attained at least some of the qualities of 'superhumanity'. Tarrying within a coarse material environment would then quickly become worthless, and even detrimental, to the purposes of further evolution. Yet 'we are all in this together', as the old saw goes, and more evolved souls may have a legitimate desire to help others. Enter the Eastern concept of *bodhisattva*, best illustrated, again, by Jane. She is a very advanced soul (why and how she has become thus being a wholly other tale.) She happens to hold multiple advanced degrees, she's radiant and generous to all, she's volunteered in a number of charities, she truly loves every soul on Earth in a way the rest of us can hardly emulate—both people and animals sense it and react accordingly, as everybody reciprocates.

On one of her field trips, Jane falls in love with Alan, a simple, solid farm boy. Alan is "salt of the Earth", and he still has a lot to learn. It will take him several incarnations to learn it all (remember that we're here within an Eastern worldview.) Jane has the option to leave the material realms firmly behind when she finally passes, but Alan hardly has that option. But she fell deeply in love, and opts to remain with him. She'll willfully pause her further upwards evolution in order to remain with Alan through his cycle of future reincarnations, and maybe her love will somehow prove helpful to him : Jane has thereby become a *bodhisattva*, an enlightened being who chose on her own accord to remain behind in this material 'vale of tears', although she did not need to. She could have 'slipped the surly bonds of Earth, and touched the face of God', in John

Magee's famous phrase, but chose temporarily not to—for the sake of love.

Should AI and transhumanism succeed in continuously lifting the bounds of possible learning experiences on Earth, then everyone, including people like Jane, would still be able to benefit spiritually from remaining behind in the material world—provided that AI and transhumanism do not somehow lessen souls, by inadvertently turning people into more or less superficial cyborg-like beings for whom learning would be of lesser spiritual value. Going out on another limb here, I'll opine that because mindstuff demonstrably takes precedence over everything and in particular all things material, there is no danger that transhumanism could somehow diminish our souls, and that on the contrary, by extending the range and limits of experience, it is well equipped to achieve the opposite. The conclusion is that transhumanism will contribute to serving the purpose of our evolution, even if a case can probably be made that whatever subtle realms there are remain the better alternative to a spiritual life, over any material environments, no matter how enhanced. Transhumanism and any other cognition- and life-enhancing technologies—some of which can presumably hardly even be foreseen at this stage—will be able, if deployed on a large scale, to impact and help everyone. Properly deployed, they will contribute to accelerating the conversion of energy that the universe is all about.

Exceptionalism, the presence in our midst of Jane-like humans with off-the-charts abilities who contribute much to the culture and the advancement of civilization, has always been with us. The personal price which, in terms of social isolation and much else besides, exceptionally gifted individuals often end up paying for allowing their talents to run free and contribute to society can sometimes be steep, and life-enhancing technologies hold out a promise that in the future the prices paid by such individuals will become much less exacting, and that no one gifted with truly exceptional talents will ever need again to recoil from the daunting price to pay, and willingly bury their talents in the sand.

Nuggets of wisdom can be found everywhere in the wheat and chaff of contemporary culture—variously hidden in the lyrics of popular music (which is why Bob Dylan received his Nobel prize in the first place, and in many other songs—listen to, say, Barclay James Harvest's song '*Who Do We Think We Are?*'), in books of every stripe, both in *nonfiction* addressing a wide variety of subjects, but also in *fiction* of all genres. As a case in point, popular author and entertainer Stephen King, whose public role is not usually viewed as that of a deep thinker, nevertheless sprinkles his work with astute observations of how life works and plays out—e.g. once observing that people may remember a particular event for years or even decades until the memory turns out to prove useful in some way and, after the memory has played its perhaps-intended role, it then promptly fades away (should we think back, we'll likely find instances of exactly that happening in our own lives); or his throwaway phrase that '*life turns on a dime*', describing the uncomfortable fickleness and unpredictability of life itself. Most religious texts also contain much wisdom, regardless of one's perspective on any particular religion, or religions in general—there is, perhaps alongside passages which reasonable people may find dubious, much wisdom in, say, the proverbs of Solomon or in the reflections in Ecclesiastes, or in the mandated duty to seek knowledge in the Quran, or the importance of self-discipline, self-realization, and selfless service in the Vedas.

The tale of the talents in the Bible, whereby three servants are given different amounts of treasure and enjoined to parlay such into more wealth and achievement, is surely one such passage. The three servants end up with quite disparate achievements—two have grown their treasure, one hasn't. Likewise, how people deploy their abilities and any innate talents they may have varies widely. We all have known people—whom we may have met again years or decades later, perhaps at class reunions—who seemed perhaps not overly gifted but who persevered, hung in there and studied doggedly and stubbornly until they achieved excellence in their chosen fields, and reversely, promising golden boys and girls—youths typically from a privileged background, before whom the usual asperities and vicissitudes of life disappeared like dew in the sun, and yet who achieved exactly *nothing* in their subsequent lives—the very folks we may have secretly admired and perhaps even envied, whom we had voted 'most likely to succeed', yet who seemingly wilted into world-class underachievers in their subsequent lives. These are the occasions when the Biblical admonition to use one's talents wisely and productively springs to mind with a vengeance : how could the golden youths of yore end up living, in the above-quoted words of author Pierre Michon, *'minuscule lives'*, when we all thought they were destined for greatness and fame, thereby also helping to keep inspiring others? Like so many others, I have seen it : the struggling student in my class who mightily grappled with his difficulties in mathematics, yet by dint of effort eventually carved out a career as a respected professor in *mathematics*, of all things. At the other end of the spectrum, John, a truly exceptionally gifted musician whom we all expected would become a world celebrity but who never achieved anything, never wrote nor recorded original music nor a soundtrack, never put out a CD or anything—despite seemingly leading a well-balanced and happy life, i.e., not wrestling with the many curveballs that life can sling, cramping styles and destroying a person's ability to work and achieve.

This is where the Bible's parable of the talents springs to mind. But because the three servants are given respectively one, three, and five 'talents' (a 'talent' was a set quantity of silver), i.e. relatively comparable amounts of starting abilities to draw from, it cannot be the whole tale : a rare few people's talents are so far beyond the norm, and the sheer scope of their achievements so great, that it beggars belief. To name but a few, it is physicist Erwin Schrödinger who works out the equation that bears his name which forms the basis upon which reality itself is understood today, it is Stephen King who writes within his lifetime a gigantic opus of well over 70 thick books and counting, every single one of which achieves best-seller status across the globe, it is Victor Hugo who, at a higher-brow level than Stephen King, pens at least 55 works including the Hunchback of Notre Dame, The Legend of the Ages, and Les Misérables (the work that spawned the longest-running musical ever in London's West End, still going strong, forty years and counting after its début in 1985), it is mathematician Evariste Galois who before the age of 20 years old revolutionizes significant swathes of mathematics and lays the foundation for essential modern-day applications such as cryptography, it is the few exceptional musicians who have pushed the envelope of what music can be, and others. In the Biblical tale of the three servants, it is as if there is an unspoken-of extra servant, who has been given several score talents rather than the somewhat measly, by that standard, one and three and five.

The way these people bring off their exceptional achievements is by busting the 'bolts' that normally keep brains under tight control. It is by now well-established that one key role of the brain is to keep a cap upon one's engagement with reality, in a way that enables and focuses the brain on its overarching evolutionary purpose : keep us alive for another day in a relentlessly dangerous world. Should the brain become damaged, this filtering function is apt to break down, which can give rise to extraordinary, well-nigh unexplainable performances : it is Akira Haraguchi, whom we've met earlier, and his championship competitors, Rajveer Meena, Suresh Sharma, Chao Lu and others, 'going into the zone' and flawlessly reeling off the number pi (π) to tens of thousands of consecutive digits, it is Jill Price's total recall of every single instant of her life since 1974, and the like achievements of many other so-called savants.

What the Mozarts and the Victor Hugos of the world, whose brains are whole and who are not savants, seem to be doing—is somehow *mirror how damaged brains work,* thereby succeeding in 'busting the brain's bolts'. And for most, being able to do so comes at a steep price, mostly hidden from view. A word of caution might be called for here—to quote the Bible again, *do not judge, lest you be judged.*

As it turns out, owing to how the human body hangs together and works, the royal road to effectively busting the bolts that would otherwise constrain the brain might be.... experiences that happen to break down all inhibitions : unbridled, often illicit sex, and/or drugs. When Victor Hugo died, the brothels of Paris closed for a day so that the prostitutes could go and attend his funeral. Erwin Schrödinger shockingly turned out to be an uninhibited pedophile, with many incidents of attempted and/or performed acting out. Evariste Galois led a dissolute personal life; he died at the age of 20 in a fight over a prostitute. Epoch-making musicians have been known to use drugs and have even composed epoch-making masterpieces in the immediate aftermath of using (a process cryptically hinted at in, for instance, the Beatles song 'Fixing a Hole'.) Some well-known musicians lost their muse after they went clean, and thereafter never again put out a masterly, unforgettable composition or record.

Nor is it a fluke : there are just too many documented cases, the very circumstance that led to the art-world adage that 'creative artists are to be judged differently'. (As a case in point—it's hard to remember now how the then extremely popular music band The Rolling Stones had helped 'change the world', in the words of its frontman Mick Jagger—inspiring youths in the then markedly hidebound West to rebel against the then pervasive priggishness and constraints of grown-up society, and youths in the communist European East to dream of freedom. The band's Keith Richards had famously stated that 'drugs are an occupational hazard for musicians', whereas Mick Jagger was known for his prodigiously unbridled sex life [xxxii], and Mick Taylor, a guitarist who had imprinted the Rolling Stones with the unique sound that helped shape some of their most successful albums, left the band in 1974 and opted for a life away from the limelight—his body could not take the drugs anymore and he, quote, 'knew that he would soon die if he carried on'.

Inevitably, owing to the extremely private nature of the phenomenon, precious few studies exist, and reliable statistics are hard to come by. If not a fluke, then the question arises as to *why* and how such excesses succeed in 'busting the bolts'—beyond simply putting the brain into an unusual state and thereby awakening a least some of its less used capabilities, and opening its doors of perception. A probably key observation here is that creativity seems to flow for a limited period of time immediately *after* the experiences that loosened and unclamped, as it were, the brain's bolts—for instance, imaginative creative fiction writers do not write at the time when the drugs hold their grip but afterwards—when the person has come down, and settles at their desk to write what then may turn out to be perfectly structured and consistent doorstop-sized novels. The same seems to hold in other pursuits. One part of the explanation may be that the brain was uncommonly stimulated—*electrified*—by the experience, leaving a residual afterglow of enhanced neurological activity for hours afterwards, which the artist taps. Another part of the explanation is suggested by the hoary cliché of construction workers good-naturedly whistling at passing beauties. The simple fact that they whistle means that their brain's 'bandwidth' remains open : they are not entirely, exclusively focused on their construction work, but their brain keeps other channels of perception at least slightly open and susceptible to instant activation, which is why they are able to catch sight of passing beauties, thereby betokening that their minds are not entirely, 100% focused on their work. It's in our evolutionary heritage : human multichannel sensory perception operates at all times. It evolved to keep an eye out for both perils and opportunities in the environment—predators, food sources, potential mates. One side effect of the massive electrical jolts that extreme experiences deliver to the brain could be to shut down extra channels for a while, perhaps to let them recover, enabling full focus on only one task at hand. Opuses of many hundred pages can then keep their taut inner consistency despite their volume and scope—a feat achieved by top fiction writers, which lesser writers sometimes find difficult to emulate.

The effect of exalted states of the brain in enhancing creativity and uncommon performance is so well documented today that people in the mainstream have been trying to generate them virtually on demand : witness the works of such pioneers as Michael Pollan, Steven Kotler, and by now many others, cautiously experimenting first with the limited and controlled use of psilocybin mushrooms and other substances, and also, tentatively and less openly, with other forms of stimulation. These pioneers seek to make high performance and achievement more readily available to anyone, ultimately well-nigh routine, virtually on demand. Observed abilities that can seem, by today's standards, extraordinarily high, sometimes border on the hard to believe. Remote viewing—a more rational-sounding name than the old-fashioned term of clairvoyance—is one such case in point. When fiction author Laurent Gounelle was researching his novel on Remote Viewing[xxxiii], he interviewed people professionally involved in the field—including one who had temporarily significantly enhanced her remote viewing abilities by using LSD—with the unforeseen consequence that she later lost much of the abilities she had worked so long to develop, as if the LSD experience had compressed and crammed all of her present and future abilities into a few short hours (Gounelle then used her profile as a character in his book.) This throws off the question, of course, of whether a statistically rare innate talent is indispensable for bolt-busting to really work, or whether anybody's skills can be, in theory at least, enhanced on demand. While Pollan's, Kotler's et al. research seem to hold out the prospect that all may benefit, a word of caution is probably called for : many people who have dabbled in mind-expanding experiments have achieved nothing out of the ordinary. Among them, some have wrecked their lives (your ordinary neighborhood junkie, for instance), and others have, try as they may, remained B- and C-listers in their chosen fields. The better part of valor seems to be, in the absence of far more research and the development of proven know-how, to '*not try this at home*'.

The world has been much enriched by the works—the literature, the music, the science—of those who end up paying a steep and sometimes terrible price for their groundbreaking contributions. There are also the Mick Taylors, who know they will pay too high a price if they keep going and try and pursue their muse, and understandably choose to let go. There are those who do *not* let go—the many musicians who died too young already (a phenomenon that has given rise to the urban legend of the 'Club of 27'[xxxiv], the mathematicians who became unhinged, including those who strove just a bit too hard to understand infinity, chronicled in the BBC series BBC series Dangerous Knowledge[xxxv], the writers who took leave of their senses primarily due to their use of mind enhancers (Edgar Allan Poe, et al.), and the question of where the morality line lies between private existential risk and tragedy versus collective commonweal is where we must turn to now.

The challenges we face today as a species are so steep and existential that we have little choice but to use any available tool—any 'arrow' in our collective quiver to tackle them, as we might not be quite bright enough at this point in our history to stave off catastrophe. Every day, we must witness the sorry spectacle of politicians whose brainboxes do not let them think outside the bounds of their narrow prejudices, we witness whole *peoples* who may be easily manipulated, as Peter Pomerantsev describes in his terrifying book[xxxvi]. Some of the issues we face seem so daunting that we may not be able to deal with them from the position of our contemporary abilities. The world would be a better—and much safer—place if we could just significantly raise the level of our collective and individual abilities. In that sense, the contributions of exceptional people to the well-being and welfare of society are more urgent than ever. Yet, most societies do not traditionally have a great track record in harnessing, for the common good, their most talented members' potential contributions. Much of the traditional notions of morality and of proper societal behavior have led to the quelling of attitudes, behaviors and people deemed deviant from the desirable, oft-enforced norms. Even in our 21st century, some societies are so feral in repressing their more talented members—the people who refuse to conform and who do not hew to the enforced groupthink or to enforced morals and strictures—that the repression they impose can amount to a frightful measure of outright *reverse Darwinism*, whereby the most creative and brightest members of society are prevented from arising, mercilessly dispensed with when they do, and thereby unsparingly taken out of their societies' gene and cultural pools.

Letting talent bloom requires freedom, and a cornerstone of freedom is that everyone, including 'disappointing' prodigies such as above-cited John, be free to lead their own lives the way they see fit. Whether John should refuse or accept to pay the personal price that may stem from giving free rein to his inborn talent must remain purely John's decision alone. Any Extra Servant—a person endowed with an immense talent needing to be set free from the fetters the brain so effectively imposes—may choose deliberately and knowingly to *not* engage with their talent. A question is whether the resulting loss to the world is, overall, the better moral option.

Those—the Victor Hugos and the musicians and all the others—who have changed and enhanced millions of lives, elevated the culture and generally brought society and its narratives forward, have often done so at a steep personal price. But isn't it the case that people routinely sacrifice for the greater good, in ways that can sometimes be harrowing? Just ask any soldier.

But we can never judge, because we can only ever judge from the outside rather than from within. The choice is never ours to make, and societies will always become better not only under freedom, but also freedom from judgment.

10 Words

Before we go back in earnest to the question of destiny in the next chapters, we must agree what the word means, and as ever the language helps with specifying and jelling thoughts. English has a number of words and phrases expressing destiny and fate, all meant to emphasize some particular angle.

'Destiny' means the full arc of a person's lived life – what they did and achieved and how they lived – irrespective of the role that the circumstances in which they were born may have played. 'Fate' on the other hand rather emphasizes the manner of their eventual demise, seen as something over which mere mortals do not have full control, because fates used to be thought of as being at least in part foreordained or 'spoken' by gods. In ancient Rome, where the word began, the 'Fates' were the three goddesses who presided over the birth and life of humans : Clotho, Lachesis, and Atropos. Their collective name 'Fates' takes its root in an old word for to 'speak' : they spoke out people's destinies, and also when called upon, oracles.

A first major contributor to anyone's ultimate fate has to be the place when and time where the person was born, and into which circumstances of family, body and wealth : 'orlay', an Old English-derived word, emphasizes the role of the circumstances of birth as a key determiner of destiny and fate. In the simpler and more primitive societies of yore, far less leeway and fewer opportunities for self-actualization existed for the vast majority who were not born into the ruling, often the warrior, classes. In the violent and hardscrabble times of bygone Europe of over a thousand years ago, the word emphasized those conditions of birth that led to destinies worth speaking of, or being sung about in minstrels' lays – a fact still reflected in Dutch, a language closely related to English, where the word has survived in its word for 'war' : '*oorlog*'. Built from the word elements *out-lay*, 'that which is laid out at the outset', the word has somewhat, if not entirely, fallen into disuse in modern English as changes in society have made its meaning less relevant.

'Wyrd' was another Old English word for fate or destiny. It emphasized 'what a person becomes', from an old word 'worth' for to 'become', still occasionally used in the set phrase '*woe worth* (a day or a person, who are thereby wished to become woe personified). Our modern 'weird' evolved from 'wyrd', because people who wanted to know what the future held in store for them went to consult the 'wyrd' people, the seers who may often have turned out to be, well, rather weird.

'Lot' also describes the overall arc of someone's passage on Earth. A person's lot is shaped by the many factors that play a role at the different stages of that person's life.

Notwithstanding the vagaries of birth, humans can only do so much to control their fate, and a big part of their lot remains out of their hands—accidents happen, history takes an unexpected turn for the worse, someone wins the lottery, and carefully and painstakingly constructed lives can unravel in seconds, and '*life turns on a dime*'. English has a quirky phrase to express the fact that whatever fate has in store for you, you have no choice but to live through it and endure it : you must '*dree your weird*', irrespective of whether your particular *weird* is due to chance and blind happenstance, or not.

In lands infused with Mohammedan culture, humans must be subservient and entirely beholden to the perceived will of God. Unsurprisingly, the concept of *maktub* rules—the notion that whatever you do, experience, deliver, is all in keeping with the will and the final arbiter and authority of God, who is solely in charge of determining and shaping lives and destinies—a role no human should ever presume to assume. The word *kismet* originated from the same culture (from Turkish, borrowed from the Arabic). It hints that a person's lot and destiny should be understood as determined by forces much bigger and wiser than that person could ever presume to be.

In turn, 'karma' came into English and many other languages from the Sanskrit : it emphasizes the fact that choices made, actions undertaken or not, roads traveled or left alone, things freely opted for and things spurned, all of that collectively determines a person's future trajectory, what and who she or he shall become, if need be over several lifetimes, until all their actions are accounted for and have been balanced out. The word derives from the Sanskrit *kr**, 'to make' – also the ultimate source of our word 'create'.

11 Individual Omegas

This brings us back to where we started, the overall issue of individual destinies. In a reality governed by laws of mathematics intermediating and enabling mindstuff into a coarser material environment, the minds of sentient beings can never just plainly disappear. Instead, they take on different forms and go through stages in which they grow and refine. Individual consciousness spikes do not simply vanish but live on and evolve, whether through some kind of temporary reincarnation or any other form of further evolution is largely immaterial —be it within environments or realms which may be hard to imagine from a limited vantage point of ordinary life on Earth. There are therefore two stages to individual destiny— a temporary cycle of serial temporary destinies where upwards individual progress is achieved piecemeal, and in the fullness of time or achievement an 'arrival zone' is attained, which in keeping with Teilhard de Chardin's terminology could be named an individual's Omega Point, the place where the individual consciousness has perfected itself. Before we look at what may happen at and beyond the Omega point, we must first look at the process leading there.

If there is growth and refinement, then there must be a beginning—an *Ur*-start to any individualized consciousness. Such a beginning can arise from a bit of consciousness separating out and detaching, either by design or by chance, from the underlying universal consciousness baseline, while of course still remaining for ever loosely networked with the rest of the panpsychic universe. The ability of consciousness to separate out or fragment has been well established clinically, so that there is nothing novel or extraordinary about this possible inception process (which would be technically indistinguishable from how 'souls are created', according to many religions.) Any hardships which sentient beings may go through would prime them for less reliance on the world of materiality, and goad them towards striving for an ever more spiritual state of being. (How the Ur-consciousness itself got its start is a wholly separate issue, which we'll revisit in a moment.)

The purpose of individual destiny is to let the person 'grow in wisdom', while contributing to the overarching goal of keeping the rest of creation (for lack of a better word) alive. There are myriad ways how individual progress can be achieved, and different people follow different paths towards that goal. Growing in wisdom in the material world can never mean becoming perfect, which not only would not even be desirable, since perfection leads to stasis and becomes counterproductive, but which also is not achievable in a material, and therefore imperfect environment. Necessary imperfection is reflected everywhere in everyday life, where choices must be made among options of which none are ever perfect—and where the better options can in many instances prove to be the riskier. As a case in point, a driving license applicant has the surprising right to make up to six mistakes out of the 30-odd questions in the multichoice exam. Since any mistake can lead to catastrophe on the road, any allowance for imperfection is objectively terrible, yet it is a necessary recognition of simple reality : if only perfect scores were admissible, there would be fewer people on the roads, which in turn would lead to a whole new raft of unintended, mostly negative consequences. In Leonard Cohen's phrase, "*There is a crack in everything, that's how the light gets in.*" As in the case of Jane we met earlier, achieving near-perfection is nature's way of telling you that it's time for you to move on and face up to new challenges.

There are many mostly irreconcilable views out there on the paths that individual destinies must take. Eastern and Western and other spiritual traditions hold different views of how individual progress can be achieved, yet the stated goal of spiritual growth is always the same, and therefore the *mechanism* of how progress is achieved is probably not of much relevance as long as the purpose is served.

The most *artistic* mechanism is that of formal religions and their accompanying bodies of unique art, in architecture, in music, and in narratives. For religions, temporary destinies unspool as per their respective canon. In most cases such may not appear overly logical—a fact acknowledged by many of their advocates, who will typically opine that the ways of divinity are impenetrable and that it's never our place to try and understand.

For some, temporary destinies are scripted. It is the view of the few religious traditions that view individual destinies as largely predetermined, such as Calvinism or Jansenism, and it is also, in part at least, the view of those who belie free will and deny any willful individual agency in how lives unfold—shaped instead by immutable imperatives beyond our ken and control. For those, light-giving cracks still exist in the guise of sheer happenstance playing an important role in life (a slightly odd situation where, in effect, sentient beings would be bereft of free agency but mechanistic nature itself would not.) Be that as it may, should we take the longer view of life as the tool by which infinity remains alive, it is hard to see how lives going robotically through rigidly scripted scenarios would contribute much, or efficiently, to an overarching goal of keeping life itself alive. A different kind of scripting is seen by those, like Robert Schwartz et al., who believe that sentient beings come to Earth after planning their forthcoming life before they are born—the key difference being that the option to either fail or exceed any goals set would then exist—in which case, much like the Bill Murray character in the 1993 movie Groundhog Day, people who fail their goals would presumably cycle back and keep trying, again and again, until they get it right and thereby become ready to move on to the next stage of their spiritual journey.

Karma, in some form or other, must be the most *logical* take on how evolutionary progress can be achieved one step up at a time. It would seem a logical way whereby individual consciousnesses can be refined and prepped for an eventual higher calling, and would provide a mechanism whereby any hindrances standing in the way of an individual's higher spiritual awareness could be dealt with, and barriers to further evolution removed. Because logic is a constituent of mathematics and ours is a mathematical universe, perhaps it should be given more credence than it is usually granted in Western culture. It can only work in the context of the ongoing existence and evolution of a person over deep time, which is why the concept of karma was first born in societies for which reincarnation is an undisputed fact of life. In Western societies, a view of karma as a reasonable possibility has become rifer over the last few decades, and accordingly regression therapy more fashionable. It tries to trace back a person's deep back history to elucidate the possible deeper causes of whatever may ail them today, paving the way towards eventual healing. A bit of a cottage industry has sprung up of therapists writing memoirs of their most intriguing cases. As in the above-cited case of Gerod, the proof of the pudding has to be as ever in the eating, the litmus criterion being whether such therapy works—which, as it turns out, it often does. Should the workings of karma be sought within a single lifetime however, it almost never works. Roland Bartetzko, a German soldier who has served in many combat situations, opines about karma that *Quote* My opinion is clear : there's no such thing as karma. It would be nice if there were, but let's not fool ourselves. Sometimes, the guy who has bad luck has been asking for it but most of the time, fate strikes completely randomly. There's no pattern. Even worse, it's often the good guys who die first. Caring about your comrade certainly is a good thing but in a combat situation, it can be extremely dangerous. On the other hand, the guys who only think about saving their own skins have a much better chance of survival. Grown-up people don't need karma tales *Unquote*. This view can only come from a place that would attempt to shoehorn karma into a single, 'three score and ten' lifetime, which on compelling grounds just cannot be the case. Imagine you'd build bad karma by being prejudiced. Your prejudices are made possible from your circumstance of not being 'one of them', and can presumably only be put right after you have become 'one of them', which of course will not happen within a single lifetime. As such, karma would not be a tool for revenge but for teaching. The Dalai Lama opined that once the necessary lesson has been learnt, and/or the habit overcome, the karma attached to it has by then fulfilled its role and, being no longer useful, just disappears. Hurting others, which most often (if not always) stems from a position of ignorance, is seen as the worst obstacle impeding spiritual progress. The way to learn then involves being put in the stead of the victim, so that the lesson to not hurt be forcefully taken on board. In the well-known Biblical phrase, sometimes interpreted differently, an eye becomes forfeited for an eye taken, and a tooth for a tooth. This could appear as an exercise in revenge, but it is not : instead, it's an exercise in *learning*.

Neither would karma be simply straightforward nor predictable. Sometimes, apparent 'bad' karma may actually stem from a long history of goodness : imagine the proverbial golden boy who sailed his way through many a kind life or existence (in one form or another), has never done anything bad. But is this past experience enough to ensure his growth in wisdom? Maybe he sorely needs a terrible incarnation, so that his mettle and depth and resilience in the face of adversity be tested? Illustrating this, people who have endured horrible childhoods—by definition through no fault of their own—react in very different ways. There is a whole roster, and counting, of people who rose over their horrible childhoods and went on to become famous and contribute much to society. Writers and musicians and actors and others, surprisingly including very famous people like author Rudyard Kipling, tortured as a child by his caregivers, composer Ludwig van Beethoven, whose deafness almost certainly stemmed from a battering by his caretakers who routinely beat him up, authors George Orwell of '1984' fame, Pat Conroy, Maya Angelou, musicians Brian Wilson of the Beach Boys, Jim Morrison of the Doors, Mary J. Blige, Johannes Brahms, Tom Petty, Christina Aguilera, Fiona Apple, Marvin Gaye, Corey Taylor, actor Chevy Chase, and so many others. And there are also those who didn't make it—John Wayne Gacy, Gary Gilmore, whose life story was later famously fictionalized and told by author Arthur Miller in his book 'The Executioner's Song', or serial killer Carl Panzram who underwent horrifying experiences in his formative years. He was later befriended by Henry Lesser, a prison guard who saw through to the person he could, and should, have become, and helped him write his memoirs before he was executed.

Nor should karma be niggling or petty. German regression therapist Thomas Hockemeyer (pen named Trutz Hardo) describes in his writings much that is more or less plausible, yet sometimes falls into places that may just be much too pat to accurately reflect how life works. As a case in point, he reports the case of a patient who saw under hypnosis a previous lifetime in which he had raped seventeen people—and who then, in order to expiate, had to undergo seventeen rapes in as many later incarnations. Perhaps a more logical view would be that any number of such experiences would keep occurring, should the person remain refractory to the lessons that must be learnt before any further progress can take place, or alternatively that only one could teach in full the lesson needed, thereby freeing up the consciousness onto the road towards further progress. Illustrating the need for extreme caution in any pat interpretation of karma, Thomas Hockemeyer landed in very hot legal waters for suggesting that the victims of World War 2 were paying the price of their accumulated bad karma—as did British football coach Glenn Hoddle for suggesting that disabled athletes in paralympic games were paying, by being disabled, a karmic price for past trespasses.

Moreover, we must bear in mind that in a mathematical universe, *mindstuff* takes full precedence over logic, and pure logic must be used with caution because it can, unexpectedly, fall short : pure logic is provably—with a '*v*', not a '*b*'—unable to resolve certain questions, and some things in life remain firmly beyond its ambit, as we'll see below. So even if karma is the most logical way by which temporary, pre-individual Omega destinies unfold, it neither follows that we understand or even can understand its workings, nor that it necessarily is the way life works all or even most of the time. In illustrating how logic can fail, we discover the intriguing fact that whereas logic, when applied to human life, can woefully fall short *before* the Omega point, it can no longer do so at Omega – illustrating the point that the further we evolve, the closer we get to the mathematical perfection of spirituality.

To illustrate how logic can fail, let us return to the everyday case of the random car number plates one may see on the street when leaving one's house. Let's say that you see three cars in a row with plates bearing the numbers 528, 529, and 530. What are the odds of seeing this number sequence? Pure logic alone *cannot* give a definite answer, because the answer depends on how your mind works – your mindstuff. Apart from the two trivial solutions either of you having thought, before you left the house, that you would come across these exact numbers in a row, in which case the odds would be one in a billion, or, you are not into numbers at all and that sequence or any other sequence of numbers does not seem in any way special to you, in which case the odds is one hundred percent (the same as that of you seeing any three numbers in a row), the picture quickly becomes fuzzier and there are a slew of different yet entirely valid answers, all of which depend on your unique mind, your mind *as it happens to be*, and two people leaving your house and seeing the very same sequence of numbers would logically lead to different probabilities of seeing that sequence, as follows.

If you left your house with no prior idea of the first numbers you'd see, the sequence of the first two numbers, made up of 528 and 529, is not particularly remarkable nor rare. Since you didn't think of any number, there is a 100% certainty that you'd see a first number, which happens here to be 528, and even if you are not specially into numbers, you'd be justified in thinking that 529 constitutes a rather neat albeit unremarkable follow-up sequence to the first number. But then 530 as the third number becomes more uniquely notable in the context of the first two numbers.

But there would also be, depending upon your own familiarity with, and even love of, numbers, other possible notable sequences that would jump out at you and look equally as special to you. Such as, maybe, the corresponding descending order—528, but then 527 and then there would be a third car with 526—or a few other sequences such as 528, 628, 728, or sequences that would skip numbers in a recognizable pattern, like 528, 548, 568, or in a slightly less immediately recognizable scheme, 528, 547, 566, and the like. If you immediately see the logical sequence in both 528, 529, 530 and in 528, 628, 728, then the odds of these series happening are, in your own mind, the exact same. If you are not much into numbers, you could probably recognize a dozen such sequences. If on the other hand you are a bit of a numbers freak, you could conceivably recognize, say, thirty thousand or so possible sequence schemes that would seamlessly associate any sequence of three consecutive three-digit numbers.

There are one billion distinct sequences of three repeatable numbers. But it so happens that *all* possible sequences are in fact related within some possible, fully legitimate mathematical scheme : for instance, 528, 001, and 067 are not obviously or visibly related but in fact they are. There is, crucially, an *infinity* of mathematical functions that can associate any three numbers, in other words any three numbers can be seamlessly associated in an infinity of logical ways, with most ways being rather involved and far from immediately obvious. (This also means that the three numbers of any sequence you'd see, including in the sequence above of 528, 001, and 067 are not only always related by a legitimate mathematical scheme, but in fact by an infinity of such schemes.) The bottom line is that logic alone is in principle unable to provide an answer as to what the mathematical odds are of the sequence 528, 529, 530 being on display outside your house and *you noticing it as an unusual sequence,* unless you had thought of this exact sequence prior : the correct odds directly depend on how many other sequences (such as 528, 525, 522) you would also recognize with the same *easiness* you recognize 528, 529, 530. The *hard* number that logic would yield entirely depends on the endlessly *soft* concept of how easily you can spot patterns in numbers. The bottom line is that pure logic cannot be depended upon to always provide incontrovertible truths—as Graham Greene had aptly put it, there is always the human factor.

As mentioned, the situation interestingly simplifies at your own Omega Point, a place where your mind has become supremely advanced and mathematically all-knowing. Whatever succession of plate numbers is on display, you now immediately recognize how these numbers can be associated within one or more valid mathematical sequences : *unless* you thought of any one specific sequence beforehand, the likelihood of *any* sequence of numbers is now never special—528, 529, 530 is then a sequence with the exact same likelihood of appearing as any other sequence such as 417, 209, 922—it is 100%. Any sequence that would appear to you to be somehow special before you reach Omega—say, three number plates in a row coincidentally all bearing the numbers 555—is now in no way special or unique. Being at your Omega point has immensely simplified all odds.

The final scene of Stanley Kubrick's 1968 film *'2001 : A Space Odyssey'*, widely held to be a or even *the* signal masterpiece of cinema, describes the astronaut character David Bowman ('Dave', played by Keir Dullea) reaching his own Omega point. The dying astronaut turns into an immaterial, glowing 'Star Child', his consciousness now risen beyond human incarnation and, presumably, incarnate cycles, uplifted to a level beyond the physical world. The final shot has the Star Child looking at Earth—maybe pondering when the rest of humankind will join, luring it to do so, or just perhaps, wondering whether to go back and help?

Omega Point is the place where any undesirable kinks have been smoothened out and all needful lessons learnt. In the fullness of time, when every consciousness has reached its own Omega

Point—where are we then, and where do we go from there? We can only speculate, and it is where we are going now.

12 Collective Omega

An across-the-board Omega point is the place where there are no more horrors, no more battered children, no more slaughterhouses, no more mind-numbing brutality, no more sentient beings left behind in the spiritual evolution sweepstakes. Whatever necessary purposes and indispensable lessons may be imparted by brutality in its many forms, it is a place where such are no longer needed. At the particular juncture in time where we find ourselves today, we are still of course nowhere near a collective Omega, yet civilization, notwithstanding its many recurrent setbacks, has already much complexified and improved. As Steven Pinker once observed, our current civilization, despite its many shortfalls, is provably leaps ahead, in just about every metric of well-being, of the achievements of previous civilizations—in quality of life, medicine, longevity, incidence of conflicts and wars, you name it. A mere few decades ago, many people shared a dream, along with Martin Luther King, that people would henceforth be judged by the content of their character rather than by the irrelevant and asinine criterion of the color of their skin. Today, despite the few occasional throwbacks, that dream has largely come true. A new dream is today afoot, evidenced by the rising background clamor on social media and current trends in sales and market shares, that our food supply will soon no longer primarily rest on the murder and torture of weaker, yet fully sentient life forms, which by rights we ought to be in the business of helping and protecting instead. There is little doubt that this dream will as well come to pass. There is of course no question that we the people need to eat, and to eat well. The science of cruelty- and murder-free nutrition already largely exists, although it sorely needs to be expanded and deepened, and much better deployed. Should we fail to do so, cruelty-free nutrition will keep falling short, as it so often does today : we are reminded here of British survival expert Bear Grylls who valiantly tried to switch to a vegan diet, which he then had to promptly forsake, because in its current patchy stage of development vegan fare was wrecking his health. Science-supported cruelty-free foodstuffs urgently need to further develop and mature, and renewed focus and efforts brought to bear in making offerings more varied and tastier, in improving distribution, production, and packaging, thereby achieving the indispensable economies of scale that will make this food industry economically appealing, while at the same time traditions and know-how and local specialties are let to develop, ultimately helping a whole new food culture rise and grow. All this can be done relatively easily, yet it's not where our collective mind space is at yet. Instead, we must still in the 21st century witness the sorry spectacle of great political shindigs serving useless or delusional or as the case may be criminal goals, to-dos complete with much braindead goose-stepping and oompah music and empty slogans, where alliances are apt to be forged with other, more or less bankrupt politicians and ways devised of variously exploiting, invading and wrecking neighboring countries. Instead, world-wide conferences could be convened at a fraction of the cost to initiate and launch collaborative science programs aiming at devising complete cruelty-free nutrition suites, and if need be Marshall-like plans to improve, boost and deploy everywhere cruelty-free food supplies. This does not even mean that we are to wholly dispense with all animal products, but it certainly says that we can do so without the horrid cost we mindlessly extract today. We are nowhere near there yet, but the many dreamers of the world believe that in time we will.

The purpose of all destinies is to return to the place where all consciousnesses ultimately belong, which we humans left eons ago, when we, in one way or another, detached from the universal consciousness in order to help out with the universe's mission of keeping infinity alive. There is no other place to which we truly belong than the more spiritual realms. Accordingly, immigrants or displaced persons who dream of going 'home' are typically disappointed if and when they finally move back to the place they idealized, in their time of exile, as their home, rediscovering the truthfulness of the old saying that one can never go home. The underlying reason why one can never go home is bigger and more subtle than simply a case of a place and a person having grown apart during a time of exile. Irrespective of which earthly place we believe we belong to, it is *not* where our home is. Like the Dave Bowman character, our true home is Omega and beyond.

Before we consider what may lie beyond a full collective Omega, there is a valid question as to whether 'every consciousness' *can* reach Omega. Separate consciousnesses may be born all the time in the form of consciousness 'bubbles' that pop up out of the universe's backdrop consciousness baseline, the way some fruit fly consciousness or equivalent can come into existence. From there on, such a bubble can evolve in two separate ways. Tiny bits of consciousness, detached from the universal baseline, can probably merge back into it, presumably as long as they have not grown past some threshold of individuation : it is conceivable that the rudimentary consciousness embedded in fruit flies could meld away back again, and its Omega point would then come in the form of the background consciousness itself reaching Omega. For more sharply delineated spikes, such as embedded in, say, a horse or a dog, it is probably much too late for that, as upward evolution to some individual Omega point must become inevitable from some threshold of consciousness.

There is also no reason why further evolution would have to necessarily take place on Earth—at latest estimate, there are no less than about twenty sextillion planets in our known universe, some of which can harbour life forms. Nor is evolution necessarily bound to take place within material (*aka* collapsed wave function types) environment types. Since there are so many ways how evolution can occur and instances of mindstuff keep on an upwards path, that we are free, within bounds, to wonder and speculate. For instance, the minds of dinosaurs were mostly extremely primitive, and they were at a bit of an evolutionary dead end. They disappeared from

Earth—but what became of their rudimentary minds? Did their minds split up into smithereens of mindstuff, into atoms of consciousness that merged back into the baseline? Did they hold on as individual spikes which, unbeknownst to us, are still alive and evolving upwards somewhere in the depths of the cosmos?

Reaching the status of full collective Omega requires the lifting of all of the background consciousness baseline to Omega—a full across-the-board rise. Whether reaching collective Omega can be performed within the 100 billion-odd years left before our universe ends is another question—and, because of the interplay between mindstuff and matter, it partly depends on us and on whichever other advanced species may exist within the universe.

Let us envision that we are at a point when collective Omega has occurred. The coarse material world no longer exists, the whole dragon has graduated into now being entirely "smoky", together with its formerly hard material 'paws' and 'tail' which by now have firmly become smoky as well, and life continues on as pure information, all of which is now contained in immaterial, "uncollapsed" quantum systems. Holevo's bound has become an artefact of the past, because no one anymore is trying to retrieve information from its quantum containers into some hard material substrate.

Does it then mean that the all-important second law of thermodynamics, which ensures the existence of differentials that enable life, can no longer operate properly, and that we risk falling into the movement-bereft stasis that would spell the end of life, along with the death of any form of Godhood that may be?

13 Beyond Collective Omega

It doesn't, because the second law of thermodynamics has a neat equivalent in the immaterial world.

There exist different sizes of infinity (usually called 'strengths' rather than 'sizes', because speaking of the size of infinities makes people, especially mathematicians, rather uncomfortable) : any given infinity at any aleph scale is infinitely bigger—stronger—than the infinity just below it, yet also infinitely smaller (*aka* "weaker") than the infinity above it. The differentials that allow for movement, and for information-based life to thrive, still exist owing to these different strengths, neither can they ever vanish, because the aleph scale is open-ended up.

Bearing in mind mathematician Keith Devlin's above-cited book-length argument that mathematics is exclusively made of relationships, the *quality* of the relationships in an environment where mathematical functions never collapse into coarser material reality, in which pure mathematics holds exclusive sway, must take on a purer, more exalted form than it does at the lower levels. These purer relationships between things that are now exclusively made up of pure mindstuff can take on a loftier quality, which happens to already have a name : in our world, it's called *love*. The less coarse universe is made up of love—an ethereal mindlike quality, ultimately so strong that it remains, at various degrees of intensity, felt throughout reality—including in coarser, more material environments.

The last mystery that must be addressed is why there is anything at all—such as the universe and ourselves, complete with whatever attendant destinies may be ours to '*dree*'—rather than just plain nothing at all.

Understanding how largely independent consciousnesses can arise and be born from the prior existence of a universal consciousness is straightforward—but what of the universal consciousness itself? The usual answer is, in essence, rather simple : it says that if nothing at all existed, then nothingness itself would be part of the things that do not exist, and we'd end up in an intractable contradiction (which can be put into strict mathematical terms, but this simple statement is the gist of what the math means.)

But this—correct—explanation is ultimately based on mathematics, itself predicated on the existence of mindstuff—and hence it becomes a bit of circular reasoning : the reason why anything exists rather than nothing is because some mind or mindstuff exists to begin with, as is needed to observe the contradiction.

The instant anything at all exists—a thought, a word, a random quantum fluctuation, a world, a universe, anything—this simple existence proves that a pure nothingness within which even the laws of mathematics would not hold can *never* have existed—nothing could exist *now* because nothing could have ever come out of a nothingness deprived of the disembodied laws of mathematics. But as we have seen, mindstuff takes precedence over mathematics. Since things do exist, a situation whereby nothing at all, meaning no mindstuff at all, would ever have existed cannot hold : in the absence of prior mindstuff, pure mathematics itself could not exist and nothing at all would exist.

But where and how did mind—or the Ur-mindstuff—originate or come to be?

A first observation is that time is implicit in the question, in its wording, 'originate', or 'come to be'. Both time and space are known to be woven into existence by quantum entanglement[xxxvii]—that is to say, by mathematics itself. To be able to exist, time, just like space, both need the prior existence of some mindstuff. The question of *how did any Ur-mind originate* then becomes circular, because what it actually reduces to is 'how did the Ur-mind give rise to itself'? I once heard an argument that Quote God is so powerful that He gave rise to Himself Unquote, which of course does not help at all : we're back to the same intractable conundrum, how can something give rise to its own existence if it does not somehow exist in the first place, to be able to do so? We also know that time is not linear, that both the past and the future can decisively affect the present. We see it in physics experiments, and likely as well in some of the many vanishingly unlikely coincidences across time that have been reported by Sharon Hewitt Rawlette and others. In delayed choice experiments, things, events and outcomes can turn out a certain way, most definitely because something, crucially inherently unpredictable at the time of the event, will happen in the future of that event. But that does not help us find an answer here, because time is created by mindstuff, irrespective of how nonlinear and bizarre and affected by events in both the future or the past it may be : should we try to shoehorn 'mindstuff' instead of 'time' in delayed choice experiments, it does not work, and we are back at sea again.

But there is actually a demonstrable, final way out of this, possibly not quite to the liking of most—as follows :

Einstein had famously stressed that no issue can be resolved from the same mindset or from the same environment that gave rise to the problem in the first place. More formally, there are incontrovertible mathematical proofs that essentially say the same thing : Kurt Gödel's incompleteness theorem, or Alfred Tarski's undefinability theorem. What it all means is that we cannot solve the issue of how mindstuff came to be *from within an environment of mindstuff*, the very environment it gave rise to, and in which we find ourselves. An understanding of how the forerunner of spacetime itself came to be (which can hardly be the proper phrase or the appropriate way of putting the question—language fails here), *can therefore only take place from somewhere outside spacetime*. As long as we are not outside of time and outside of space, it is demonstrably impossible to tease out any answer to the ultimately cause or causes of time and space. We can push back the limits of understanding, a job physics does, as so very often, superbly :

Time and space come from entanglement,

and

Entanglement comes from mathematics,

and

Mathematics comes from mindstuff.

And that is where it stops, and we can go no further.

The last piece of knowledge or understanding is *in principle* closed to us as long as we reside inside spacetime, which we do : understanding *whence mindstuff?* is an intrinsically unsolvable problem.

We have nevertheless determined that there is a higher, never-ending hierarchy of subtler and subtler realms both within our individual and collective destinies. Because subtler realms demonstrably hold more information than can ever be known or accessed from within a coarser environment, such subtler realms are therefore, in a universe where information is ultimately the only reality, also more 'real'. We are nowhere near there yet, but it is where we'll eventually arrive. How fast we do so, both individually and collectively, is entirely up to us.

Further Reading

A short selection of books contributory to this book's themes.

Adam, David. The Genius Within. Picador, 2018.

Al-Khalili, Jim, and McFadden, Johnjoe. Life on the Edge : The Coming of Age of Quantum Biology. Bantam Press, 2014.

Albert, David Z. After Physics. Harvard University Press, 2015.

Anderson, Christopher. Mick : The Wild Life and Mad Genius of Mick Jagger. Gallery Books, 2012.

Balcombe, Jonathan. What a Fish Knows. Farrar, Strauss & Giroux, 2017.

Bloom, Howard. Global Brain. John Wiley, 2000.

Braithwaite, Victoria, 'Do Fish Feel Pain?' Oxford University press, 2010

Broinowski, Anna. Datsun Angel : A True-Story Adventure Inside the Savage Heart of 1980s Australia. Hachette Australia, 2024.

Cahalan, Susannah. Brain on Fire. Simon & Schuster, 2013.

Challenger, Melanie. How To Be An Animal : What it Means to Be Human. CanonGate, 2020.

Darling, David & Banergee, Agnijo. Weird Math : At the Edge of Infinity and Beyond. Harper Collins 2018.

Darling, David & Banergee, Agnijo. Weirdest Math : At the Frontiers of Reason. OneWorld Publications, 2021

Darling, David & Banergee, Agnijo. The Biggest Number in the World. OneWorld Publications, 2022.

Davies, Paul. The Demon in the Machine. University of Chicago Press, 2019.

Devlin, Keith. The Math Gene. Basic Books, 2001.

de Wall, Frans. Mama's Last Hug : Animal Emotions. W.W. Norton, 2019.

Doidge, Norman. The Brain That Changes Itself. Viking, 2007.

Eagleman, David. Livewired. CanonGate Books, 2020.

Gann, Ernest K. Fate is the Hunter. Simon & Schuster, 1986.

Gao, Shan. The Meaning of the Wave Function. Cambridge University Press, 2017.

Godfrey-Smith, Peter. Other Minds. Farrar, Straus and Giroux, 2016.

Goff, Philip. Consciousness and Fundamental Reality. Oxford University Press, 2017.

Gounelle, Laurent. Intuitio. Calman Lévy, 2021.

Hand, David J. The Improbability Principle. Farrar, Strauss & Giroux, 2014.

Harley, Trevor. The Science of Consciousness. Cambridge University Press, 2021.

Heller, Michael, and Woodin, Hugh, eds. Infinity : New Research Frontiers. Cambridge University Press, 2011.

Hoffmann, Dirk. Grenzen der Mathematik. Spektrum Akademischer Verlag, 2011.

Jinks, Tony. Disappearing Object Phenomenon McFarland & Company, 2016.

Jung, Carl Gustav. Memories, Dreams, Reflections. Vintage Books (re-issue), 1989.

Kanigel, Robert. The Man Who Knew Infinity. Scribner's, 1991.

Karikó, Katalin. Breaking Through : My Life in Science. Crown, 2023.

Klaas, Brian. Fluke : Chance, Chaos, and Why Everything We Do Matters. Scribner, 2024.

Knight, Sam. The Premonitions Bureau. Faber & Faber, 2022.

Kotler, Steven. The Rise of Superman. New Harvest Books, 2021.

Kotler, Steven. Stealing Fire. Dey Street Books, William Morrow, 2017.

Kushner, Harold. 'When Bad Things Happen to Good People', Schocken Books, 1981

Kripal, Jeffrey. The Superhumanities. University of Chicago Press, 2022.

Kripal, Jeffrey. How to Think Impossibly. University of Chicago Press, 2024.

Lane, Nick. The Vital Question. Profile Books, 2016.

Montgomery, Sy. The Soul of an Octopus : A Surprising Exploration into the Wonder of Consciousness. Atria Books, Simon & Schuster, 2015.

Moody, Raymond. Paranormal : My Life in Pursuit of the Afterlife. Harper One, 2012.

Morris, Simon Conway. Life's Solution : Inevitable Humans in a Lonely Universe. Cambridge University Press, 2004.

Moss, Robert. Active Dreaming. New World Library, 2011.

Nelson, Roger. Connected : The Emergence of Global Consciousness. ICRL Press, Princeton, 2019.

Nott, David. War Doctor : Surgery on the Front Line. Picador, 2019.

Pachirat, Timothy. Every Twelve Seconds. Yale University Press, 2013.

Päs, Heinrich. The One. Basic Books, 2023.

Penrose, Roger. Cycles of Time. The Bodley Head, 2010.

Penrose, Roger, ed. Consciousness and the Universe : Quantum Physics, Evolution, Brain & Mind. Cosmology Science Publishers, Cambridge MA. 2017

Percival, Rob. The Meat Paradox. Pegasus Books, 2022.

Pinker, Steven. The Better Angels of Our Nature. Penguin Books, 2012.

Pollan, Michael. How to Change Your Mind. Penguin Press, 2018.

Pomerantsev, Peter. How to Win an Information War. Public Affairs 2024.

Ransford, H Chris. In search of Ultimate Reality : Inside the Cosmologist's Abyss. Ibidem Press, 2020.

Ransford, H Chris. You Are Fundamental. Ibidem Press, 2022. Foreword by Harley, Trevor.

Rawlette, Sharon Hewitt. The Source and Significance of Coincidences. Sharon Hewitt Rawlette, 2019.

Ring, Kenneth. Heading Toward Omega. Harper Perennial, 1985

Rodrigues dos Santos, Jose. O Jardim dos Animals com Alma. Gradiva Publicaçôes s.a., 2021.

Safina, Carl. Alfie and Me : What Owls Know, What Humans Believe. W.W. Norton, 2023.

Safina, Carl. Beyond Words : What Animals Think and Feel. Picador, 2016.

Schlanger, Zoë. The Light Eaters : The New Science of Plant Intelligence. 4th Estate, 2024.

Sinclair, Upton. The Jungle. Ancient Wisdom Publications (Reprint), 2018.

Stout, Martha. The Myth of Sanity. Viking, 2001.

Tammet, Daniel. Born on a Blue Day. Free press, 2007.

Tegmark, Max. Life 3.0 : Being Human in the Age of Artificial Intelligence. Efinito, Penguin 2017.

Tegmark, Max. Our Mathematical Universe. Knopf, 2014.

Teilhard de Chardin, Pierre. The Phenomenon of Man. Harper Perennial, 1959.

Vedral, Vlatko. Decoding Reality. Oxford University Press, 2010.

Vilenkin, Alexander. Many Worlds in One. Farrar, Strauss & Giroux. 2006

Weir, Wendy. In the Spirit. Harmony Books, 1999.

White, Christopher. Other Worlds : Spirituality and the Search for Invisible Dimensions. Harvard University Press, 2018.

Wohlleben, Peter. The Hidden Life of Animals : Love, Grief, and Compassion : Surprising Observations of a Hidden World. Greystone Books, 2017.

Wróbel, Szymon ed. Atheism Revisited : Rethinking Modernity and Inventing New Modes of Life. Palgrave Macmillan, 2020.

Yaffa, Eliach. Hasidic Tales of the Holocaust. Oxford University Press, 1982.

Yanofsky, Noson. The Outer Limits of Reason : What Science, Mathematics, and Logic Cannot Tell Us. MIT Press, 2016.

Acknowledgments

Books are never written in a vacuum, but are made possible by the vast ecosystem of thinkers, artists, thought leaders and, to use a Neil Young phrase, the ordinary people and commonfolk who have come before and who provide the necessary backdrop from whence new insights and novel ways of looking at things may arise. In that sense, I am deeply indebted to way too many people to mention. To all of them – thank you.

At Ibidem Press, my heartfelt thanks go to the whole team and especially to Laurin Orth, who went above and beyond the call of duty to efficiently deliver this book within very tight deadlines. Laurin, it was a blessing to have you there.

Finally, to my extraordinary family who have selflessly supported my ventures throughout the years, thank you. I love you all.

About the Author

H Chris Ransford grew up in several countries, which left him fluent in several languages. He was a guest Academic at the Karlsruhe Institute of Technology in Germany on a DAAD scholarship, a Research Fellow and tutor at both Monash University and the University of Melbourne in Australia. He holds a '*Grande Ecole*' engineering degree from INPG/Phelma in France. He published '*The Far Horizons of Time*' with de Gruyter (2015), '*God and the Mathematics of Infinity*' (Ibidem Press and Columbia University Press, 2017), '*In Search of Ultimate Reality : Inside the Cosmologist's Abyss*' (Ibidem Press and Columbia UP, 2019) and '*You Are Fundamental*', with a foreword by Trevor Harley (Ibidem Press, 2022). He occasionally contributes other pieces, including Conference Papers, articles as well as a Chapter in the anthology '*Atheism Revisited*' edited by Szymon Wrobel (Palgrave Macmillan 2020). A trailing spouse, he makes his home in both Melbourne and Washington DC, and still deplores the fact that smiles are no longer welcome on passport pictures.

End Notes

i See also https://globalbraininstitute.org/.)

ii Monastyrsky, Mikhail. "Modern Mathematics in the Light of the Fields Medals", A.K. Peters Ltd, 1998, pp. 101-102

iii See also https://socialstudieshelp.com/how-language-influences-our-worldview-and-perception/

iv Albert, David Z. 1994, Ransford, H Chris. 2020 et al. describe at popular science level the physics that underlies the observer effect. At a more technical level, see e.g. Cohen-Tannoudji, Claude. 2019 ed., Merzbacher, Eugen. 1997, Schiff, Leonard. 1968, Gao, Shan. 2017, and Albert, David Z. & Ney, Alyssa. eds. 2013

v See e.g. Eagleman, David. 2020.

vi Gao, Shan. "*What is it Like to Be a Quantum Observer, and What Does it Imply About the Nature of Consciousness?*" at : http://philsci-archive.pitt.edu/14836/1/feels%20v999.pdf

vii Ransford, H Chris. 2022

viii The concept of mindstuff has been addressed in a number of publications, some of which are listed here. The term may be used to describe the agency within the mind that perceives or feels or carries out mental actions such as mental arithmetic or similar. At its most basic, "mindstuff" is the irreducible awareness, the abiding *essence* that underlies any given consciousness, irrespective of that consciousness's temporary capabilities, independently of its actions and of any performance which it may be able to deploy or act out. For instance, Susannah Calahan describes in her book 'Brain on Fire : My Month of Madness' the extreme and harrowing personality changes she underwent as a result of a rare brain contamination, which resulted in her behaving as a totally different person : although she *appeared* to have become someone else, her irreducible mindstuff provided, throughout the different stages of the ailment and the resulting personality changes she underwent, the continuity which enabled her to remain an uninterrupted and full observer of her experience and later report on it. Irreducible mindstuff, independent of the brain's machinery, is revealed as well, variously, in Cat Marnell's memoirs, in which she reports that she could not make any sense at all of the mathematics she was studying in class, a subject in which kept earning D grades or worse, *until* she started taking Ritalin, whereupon she became a quite effortless straight-A math student; yet, both when and when not able at math, she definitely remained the same person throughout. It is also artists who put out seminal works and then somehow lose their muse and become mediocre, whose mindstuff remains nevertheless whole, separate as it is from the outward markers of the machinery of the brain, its performance and its cognition. It is the underlying essence that stays back from and witnesses all of life's many changes. The Eastern concept of reincarnation, whether factual or not, provides a great illustration : mindstuff as the spike of consciousness that endures regardless of experiences made, capabilities, circumstances, and under that Eastern view, of bodies temporarily inhabited. In panpsychism, mindstuff is the only reality, giving rise directly and indirectly to everything else that is, as we shall see.

ix See e.g. Vilenkin, 2006

x On split personalities, see e.g. Stout, Martha. 2001. Also Zinser, Thomas. 'Soul-Centered Healing', Union Street Press, 2011

xi For plants, see Zoë Schlanger, 2024

xii see also the conclusion at https://www.ncbi.nlm.nih.gov/pmc/articles/PMC8175961/ and other refs which looks at intriguing theoretical possibilities.). Barron & Klein 2016 https://www.wellbeingintlstudiesrepository.org/animsen t/vol1/iss9/1/. See also : https://www.sciencedirect.com/science/article/abs/pii/S0168159121002197

xiii See Roger Nelson's Global Consciousness Project.

xiv Sheldrake, Rupert. A new science of life, 2009 Edition (revised from the original 1995 edition), Faber & Faber

xv See https://www.tylervigen.com/spurious-correlations

xvi Goff, Philip. 2017.

xvii Immanence or Transcendence? A Mathematical View : https://philpapers.org/rec/RANIOT-11

xviii In fiction, see popular novels such as '*Maybe in Another Life*' by Reid, Taylor Jenkins or '*The statistical probability of Love at First Sight*' by Smith, Jennifer etc. In nonfiction, Rawlette 2019. also Richo, David. The Power of Coincidence, Shambhala Books 2007 and others.

xix Ref also https://www.space.com/whats-beyond-universe-edge. Also Ransford, H Chris. 2020, which presents an argument based on the Born rule and reviews possible objections.

xx Kushner, Harold. 1981.

xxi Knight, Sam. 2022

xxii See Paul Broks's piece at https://www.theguardian.com/world/2023/apr/13/are-coincidences-real

xxiii See previous note and Hand, David J. 2014

xxiv Rawlette, Sharon Hewitt. 2019

xxv Eliach, Yaffa. 1982

xxvi Nott, David. 2019

xxvii Balcombe, Jonathan. 2016 , also Braithwaite, Victoria. 2010 xxviii See e.g. Pachirat, Timothy. 2013. *Warning, these references contain distressing material.* Among a slew of other such resources : https://www.bbc.com/news/stories-50986683 https://www.thedoe.com/2020/06/01/inside-a-slaughterhouse/ and https://www.huffpost.com/entry/meet-the-former-slaughter_b_10199262 https://newsroom24x7.com/2016/08/07/directly-from-the-slaughterhouse/ Eisnitz, Gail. Slaughterhouse. Prometheus Books, 1997.

xxix Percival, Rob. 2022.

xxx See also https://www.theguardian.com/books/2018/oct/10/growing-up-in-a-house-full-of-books-is-major-boost-to-literacy-and-numeracy-study-finds

xxxi Penrose, Roger. 2010

xxxii Anderson, Christopher. 2012

xxxiii Gounelle, Laurent. 2021

xxxiv See e.g. https://www.dclibrary.org/news/27-club-deeper-dive-tragic-phenomenon

xxxv BBC series 'Dangerous Knowledge' https://www.imdb.com/title/tt1520274/

xxxvi Pomerantsev, Peter. 2024

xxxvii See e.g. : https://www.nature.com/articles/527290a https://www.annualreviews.org/doi/full/10.1146/annurev-conmatphys-033117-054219 https://www.wired.com/2016/01/quantum-links-in-time-and-space-may-form-the-universes-foundation/ https://thewire.in/science/quantum-mechanics-entangled-time , https://www.quantamagazine.org/how-space-and-time-could-be-a-quantum-error-correcting-code-20190103/